OFF THE RAILS
IN PHNOM PENH

OFF THE RAILS IN PHNOM PENH

INTO THE DARK HEART OF GUNS, GIRLS, AND GANJA

Amit Gilboa

ASIA BOOKS

This book exists only through the efforts of many people. I would like to thank the following individuals for their advice and encouragement: David Bamberger, Richard Baker, Ben Bradford, Tom Cakuls, Arlyn Gilboa, Nisan Gilboa, Allison Hastings, Jason Hodin, Laura Modlin, Steve Nixon, and Heike Uhlig.

Above all, this book is dedicated to Noam, who is more important than he knows.

Published and distributed by
Asia Books Co. Ltd.,
5 Sukhumvit Road Soi 61,
PO Box 40,
Bangkok 101 10,
Thailand.
Tel: (662) 714 0740-2 ext. 221-223
Fax: (662) 381 1621, 391 2277

Cover photograph by Olivier Pin-Fat
Photographs by Amit Gilboa

Typeset by COMSET
Printed by Darnsutha Press Ltd.

ISBN 974-8303-34-9

Contents

Prologue

All the events depicted in this book are real. All the characters are based on actual people whom I met between August 1996 and April 1998. The book contains only those incidents which I witnessed personally or which were reported to me from reliable sources. Real names and some place names have been changed to protect identities and to suit the narrative flow. I took three measures to ensure the accuracy of everything which I did not witness personally. First, I concealed the fact that I was writing a book in order to avoid people exaggerating in the hope of finding themselves in print. Second, I would often ask questions about a story that had been related to me weeks or even months before, to check if responses had changed—a good indication of falsehood. Finally, on those occasions when I did field research of my own, I was able to witness many of the things I had heard about. I found that, if anything, my friends and acquaintances actually understated their experiences rather than exaggerated them. I also had a very strong feeling that these people were not lying. The utter shamelessness of the group meant that there was no reason to censor oneself. The fact that fantastic stories were so freely available to all meant that there was no incentive to engage in one-upmanship. Sundry newspaper articles and other sources also helped confirm the information from my respondents. Those few individuals who had a tendency to exaggerate were easily identified, and I have not included stories from them that could not be corroborated by myself or more reliable sources.

In reading through this book, the reader may find it implausible that a) people would really engage in the activities described, and b) that they would talk about them so freely and explicitly. Addressing the latter first; even more fascinating than what they did, was the openness with which they talked about their activities. Usually, obtaining good information from interviews requires an initial period of trust and relationship-building. Such efforts are not necessary in Phnom Penh. Indeed, anyone who looks suitably unlike a Christian fundamentalist can listen to similar conversations to those I heard within an hour of arriving in Cambodia. Additionally, the people I spoke with seemed to make no effort to hide any detail, no matter how disturbing, in order to maintain some facade of 'decency' (whatever that may be). As to the first question, Phnom Penh is conclusive proof of the ancient cliché that fact is stranger than fiction.

While this book is a work of non-fiction and is meant to be informative as well as entertaining, it in no way represents an exhaustive study of the topics covered. I encourage interested readers to consult any of the books listed in the bibliography for authoritative information on any of the issues discussed in the book.

Although non-fiction, this book is not representative of the general expatriate population in Cambodia. The reader should keep in mind that most foreigners and the majority of Khmers (ethnic Cambodians) in Phnom Penh lead 'decent,' ordinary lives, often in quite difficult circumstances. This book specifically focuses on those people in Phnom Penh that live (as judged by 'normal' Westerners) 'indecent' and extraordinary lives. Even though the following are not mentioned in this book, I ask the reader to remember that there are foreigners in Phnom Penh who do not purchase sex, there are Khmers in Phnom Penh who do not carry grenades, and there are days in Phnom Penh when you will not hear gunfire.

Because it is impossible to represent the Khmer language with any measure of accuracy in English letters, I have chosen simply to use English letters that, when read by the average Western reader, produce the closest approximation of Khmer speech. For example, although the usual spelling of the Khmer Republic's leader is *Lon Nol*, in the original Khmer there is a very clear distinction between the *o* in his first name (which rhymes with *spoon*) and the *o in* his last name (which rhymes with *ball*). Therefore, I spell his name as *Loon Nol*. Similarly, I refer to the country of Vietnam as its inhabitants do, i.e. with two words—*Viet Nam*. However, I bow to the conventions of English and spell the adjective using one word—*Vietnamese*.

Finally, a brief word about Cambodia itself. It is a land where the depth and beauty of the people and culture are matched only by the depth and enormity of the people's sufferings. This book was neither conceived nor written as an appeal to conscience regarding that tortured country. Nevertheless, I would still like to remind readers of the constant suffering of Cambodians at the hands of poverty, violence, corruption, landmines, preventable disease, and countless other man-made calamities.

In the July 1993 elections, the Cambodian people braved intimidation and adversity in order to demonstrate their overwhelming support for peace and democracy. They deserve better than what they have received.

Impressions

"Cambodia is like you're always tripping."

Phnom Penh is an anarchic festival of cheap prostitutes, cheap drugs, and frequent violence. And it is all set against a backdrop of the most stunning architecture, beautiful music, and wretched political history on the planet. For an individual coming from a modern Western society, it is a city where the immoral becomes acceptable and the insane becomes normal. Despite having lived in several major cities in America, Asia, and the Middle East, throughout my time in Cambodia, I was confronted with a world more absurd and more unbelievable than I had ever experienced. Cambodia continually challenged my conception of what is real and what is impossible. I discovered an entire street devoted to wooden shack brothels, where the girls are available for $2, and restaurants where marijuana is the favored topping for the pizzas. I heard tales of political intrigue, violence, and corruption that make the Mafia look like the Rotary Club in comparison.

Of course, there was little in Cambodia that was entirely new to me. I had personally witnessed violent crime in Washington DC, political repression in China, dissolute expats in Saigon, prostitution in Bangkok, squalor in Manila, and all manner of human excess in New York City. But none of these, nor even all of them combined, could prepare me for the riot of absurdities and immoderation which awaited me in Phnom Penh.

1

Off the Rails in Phnom Penh

That I was in Cambodia at all that sunny day in September was a fortunate accident. Two months earlier, I had left my home in Pittsburgh for Viet Nam, to embark on what I hoped would be a fascinating and lucrative career in journalism. I began writing for business magazines in Ho Chi Minh City, covering the feverish expectations and constant tribulations of foreign investors eager to get in on "the next tiger economy." In my first two months in Viet Nam, I had written some competent articles, and had also used up my initial visa. It was time for a visa run. This is the process of removing oneself from Viet Nam in order to obtain a new visa, and then return. The easiest place to do the visa run is Phnom Penh, and thus it was that my eyes were opened to this incredible country and the foreigners who make it their home.

An English teacher I met summed it up best when she said that, "Cambodia is like you're always tripping." The assault on my sensibilities began on my first day in Phnom Penh. I spent the day in a low-budget restaurant, eavesdropping and occasionally chatting with expatriate residents of the city. In their casual, everyday conversations, they made countless references to drugs, sex, and violence which topped anything I had heard before. Whether compared to sex tourists in the Philippines, or drugged out backpackers in Goa, the Phnom Penh residents reached new frontiers in shock value. They talked explicitly of their exploits in brothels as if describing a day at work. They spoke of taking heroin like it was drinking coffee. They talked of gunfire and crime as if they were talking about the weather. It seemed that they had completely let go of whatever moral and societal inhibitions had elsewhere restrained them, and had simply run amok in Phnom Penh.

Almost immediately, I became committed to the idea of investigating this madhouse of a country and its foreign-born inmates. I wanted to understand the details of this country which seemed to consist entirely of the perversion of what would be called 'normal' in many other societies. I also wanted to understand the attractions that this country held for the people who chose to come here to live. Finally, I was deter-

2

mined to successfully relate all of this to those who have never been to Cambodia.

Between September 1996 and October 1997, I made several more trips to Phnom Penh, each time taking about a month off from my less-than-explosive journalistic career in Viet Nam. The standard place to eat and sleep for backpackers, low-budget visa runners, and also many longer-term residents in Phnom Penh is the sadly misnamed Majestic Restaurant and Guesthouse. During my visits I spent my time, using the Majestic as a base, learning about a range of extraordinary lifestyles from the people who were actually living them. I talked with them over quick breakfasts before their classes, and over long lunches before their brothel trips. I listened quietly as they talked in groups, and I interviewed them earnestly one on one.

Most of my conversations revolved around the sensationalistic aspects of living in Phnom Penh, and all of these are addressed throughout this book covering: The bizarre political system, and the anarchy and violence that result; the permissiveness and recklessness regarding sex, AIDS, and drugs; the ease with which the foreigners earn money from the Khmers; some interesting observations about the foreigners of Phnom Penh; and observations on the Khmers themselves. While these chapters detail the more outrageous aspects of life in Phnom Penh, there are other, more subtle facets of living in the Kingdom of Cambodia that make it a mind-altering experience. It was these subtleties, as much as the sex, drugs and violence, that entranced me to Cambodia.

Khmer culture undeniably accommodates one of the world's greatest artistic traditions. I've been past the Royal Palace in Phnom Penh hundreds of times, and it never ceases to amaze me. The beautiful colors, the intricate patterns, the four giant faces looking out from the top of the central tower. It's as if, just by appreciating it, I'm somehow a part of this monumental culture.

As millions of tourists and travelers will attest, the massive size and incredible artistry of Angkor Wat, the country's greatest monument, is an easy way to understand the glory of the Khmer Empire and the cultural heights it reached. But the strength of Khmer culture is not limited to monuments. I have traveled all around East Asia and the popular radio stations play American rock and roll, or dreadful local imitations of American rock and roll. Cambodia is the first Asian country I have been to where I actually heard mostly traditional music. And the music itself is so beautiful, the way they slide up and down the scale, all in these mournful minor keys. The very traditional music is played on an ensemble of musical instruments including gongs, bells, drums, and various other string and percussive pieces. As a person not usually given to romanticizing 'exotic' cultures, I was totally unprepared for the effect this strange and exquisite music has on me. Whenever they start playing, I always feel as if some part of me is being transported to a mythical Angkorian kingdom of princes, warriors, dancers, and gods.

The clash between this traditional culture and the modern world is part of the energy of Phnom Penh. A journalist remarks that, "This is a society that's been through hundreds of years of agrarian feudalism, twenty-three years of civil war, ten years of Communism and isolation, ten years of foreign occupation, and then the world just flipped a switch and turned Cambodia into this democratic, capitalistic, open, developing country. You think there might be some tension created?"

The fact that the process of Cambodia's 'development' is still in the early stages is clearly an attraction for many. One is constantly jarred by the contrasts. Wealthy generals drive by in Landcruisers or BMW's flanked by bodyguards, past cyclo (three-wheeled pedicab) drivers who own nothing but the cyclo and one change of clothes. While the generals own two or three villas, the cyclo drivers actually live in their cyclos because they can't even afford to rent an $8-a-month shanty. There is an overwhelming rawness that confronts the visitor; the trash in the streets, the little children running around naked, the dust, the unpaved roads, and the shacks. And amongst all of this one regularly chances upon a beautiful *wat* (Buddhist temple) rising up into the sky. While stunning in its own right, the sight is even more amazing in the middle of all the shit that surrounds it.

The Cambodian countryside provides the visitor with another perspective. A motorcycle ride only a few minutes outside Phnom Penh reveals long stretches with no brick or stone structures in sight; just wooden shacks, rice fields, and incredible 100-foot sugar palms. I always enjoy meeting Khmers in the countryside with their bright smiles and warm eyes. Yet, no matter how much of their language I learn, I always feel that behind those eyes are people so radically different from me that the communication gap can never be bridged in anything but the most superficial level. "Agrarian" or "pre-industrial" are polite words with which to describe Khmer peasants. But, in spite of the negative connotations it carries, the word which often springs to mind is "primitive."

The impressions above are more or less in line with what one might expect from travelers to Cambodia. But Cambodia holds other surprises for the visitor. For example, I was sitting eating breakfast at a street stall one morning and became very confused because I heard someone singing the prayer chant for Yom Kippur, the Jewish Day of Atonement. It turns out there was a wedding nearby, and that it was a traditional Khmer wedding chant. But it sounded very, very similar to the Yom Kippur prayers. As I began to learn Khmer, I noticed many Khmer letters with identical or nearly identical counterparts in the Hebrew alphabet. And in both languages, the vowels are under, next to, or above the consonants. The odd coincidences do not stop with the language; the wedding costumes of Yemenite-Jewish weddings are very similar to Khmer wedding attire, and the ubiquitous Khmer scarf—the *kromah*—is almost identical to the Arab *kaffiyeh*. While I wouldn't claim to have found the Ten Lost Tribes, these coincidences, especially among the other surreal aspects of Cambodia, were fascinating as well as vaguely unsettling.

Similarly, many people cite their own bizarre reasons for finding Cambodia so interesting. A long conversation I had with a tourist provided the initial idea for the the subtitle for this book. He expounded about why Phnom Penh is nothing

5

less than a real-life version of the movie *Apocalypse Now*. "Think about it, *Apocalypse Now* and *Heart of Darkness* [the Joseph Conrad novel on which the movie is based], are built on the premise of what happens when people live without the normal restraints of society. That's exactly what we're seeing here. The foreigners here have absolutely nothing stopping them from behaving completely irrationally, and completely without judgment or inhibitions. I'm telling you, it's no coincidence that they put Colonel Kurtz in Cambodia."

An NGO (non-governmental organization) worker from Australia is "blown away" by—of all things—the North Korean Embassy. He elaborates; "Cambodia's relationship with North Korea is unique because of the long-standing friendship and continuous support that King Sihanouk has received from North Korean leaders. To this day, the King's bodyguards are North Korean. The North Korean Embassy is a grand building, but what's most interesting is the photograph display board on the outside wall. The display—and they have these in Vientiane also—is updated monthly, each time with a new theme—the love of the people for the departed 'Great Leader,' or the incredible advancements in North Korean science and technology, etc.

"Last month's display was totally surreal. There's a series of pictures of that pudgy little turd [Kim Jong-Il, North Korea's new 'Dear Leader'] in various military situations. In one, he's looking confused as this group of generals explain tactics under a camouflage net. Then he's reviewing troops, and they managed to capture his face in this expression like he's sneezing and farting at the same time. In this other one he's clumsily handling an assault rifle and the fatigues give you a perfect view of his outrageous pot belly. No pictures of the people eating grass and dying of starvation."

Finally, in an unintended irony, many foreigners are fascinated by the other foreigners. Cambodia is so disorganized that anyone can, and does, arrive as a tourist or entrepreneur. I was consistently surprised by the variety of nationals I encountered in Phnom Penh. Within the first few weeks of my first visit I met Burmese, Thais, Malays, Vietnamese, Chinese from all over Asia, a Cameroonian, a Zairian, Sri Lankans, a Tunisian, Iranians, an Afghani, and of course, Europeans from every corner of the continent. I had never expected to meet an Afghani, especially an Afghani running Phnom Penh's first office supply mail-order catalog service?

One Canadian woman offers an example of this Phnom Penh melting pot. She shares a house with a teacher who is living with an ex-brothel-worker (Vietnamese) and another teacher married to one of his (Khmer) students. She tells me of the night she, "Came home to find three Indonesian sailors on shore leave who'd bought out three Vietnamese prostitutes from a brothel. The girls asked these obliging seamen to stop by their friend's [the Vietnamese girlfriend of the teacher] house, which is also my house. So, this gang of six— the three Indonesian sailors and the three Vietnamese prostitutes—came to visit their eighteen-year-old Vietnamese prostitute friend who's living with a forty-year-old Irishman who's sharing a house with two Canadians, and a Swede who has a daughter with his Khmer wife. My friend's girlfriend gets to see her friends, and the sailors get to be a part of their dates' everyday lives as if they were having real relationships and weren't just pathetic losers renting cheap prostitutes for the night. And I get to watch this comedy of the absurd called Cambodia."

As the following journal excerpts show, my own impressions corroborate other people's assessments about the wonder of Cambodia.

Overland to Phnom Penh
October 20, 1996

While I did the visa run by airplane, I do the rest of my visits overland. This is much cheaper than flying, and allows me to see the countryside as well. To get from Saïgon to the border for my first overland trip, I take a minibus operated by a backpacker-oriented travel agency in Saigon. We are an unremarkable group of tourists watching Viet Nam's remark-

7

able green scenery roll by. After a couple of photo stops and thousands of rice fields, we are finally at the drop off point for those going to Cambodia. I am the only one to disembark. Braving the onslaught of Honda om's (motorcycle taxis), I enter negotiations with one of the drivers. Laughing at his ridiculous but hardly surprising attempt to overcharge me, I instead hand over the proper fare of 10,000 dong (90 cents). He reluctantly accepts the money and we set off for the border. My excitement builds as we approach Cambodia; a sign warns that we are ENTERING FRONTIER AREA. Although we are still in Viet Nam, I see people wearing kromahs (the traditional Khmer scarf) around their heads and necks, and I begin noticing storefront signs written in Khmer script.

We finally reach the border crossing, and I get off the scooter. Standing inside Viet Nam's border gate, I can peer across the no man's land into Cambodia for a view of the Cambodian post. Viet Nam's Soviet-inspired concrete building is in sharp contrast to the classical Angkor Wat motif of the Cambodian checkpoint. The scripts on the buildings provide another study in contrasts. Vietnamese is written in Roman characters, with a lot of accent symbols around the vowels indicating pronunciation and tone. It is practical and, for the Westerner, the Roman characters make it relatively easy to learn. But with all those accent marks crawling around, it can hardly be described as beautiful. Across the no man's land, I see the text on the Cambodian gate. The Khmer letters are rendered in flowing lines with mysterious, beckoning curves. My impression of the script is that it is ancient and noble. It looks to me as much an excuse to paint as a way to communicate.

I enter the checkpoint hall on the Vietnamese side, and am completely unsurprised to run into problems right away. I had already gone to the Immigration Department in Saigon to plead and pay for the special permission required to leave the country overland. Thus, I pass the visa desk with relative ease. The customs desk is where they get me.

"Where your customs declaration form?" the official asks. He must be referring to some piece of paper that I have either

8

never received or (more likely) long since lost. As I shake my head, the official delivers what is clearly his favorite line; "OK, you go back Saigon." He knows very well that it is a three hour ride, that all I want to do is to leave this damn country, and that by not letting me through he is costing me at least three extra days in Viet Nam and who knows how much expense and headache straightening out whatever meaningless triviality needs to be straightened out. But that is fine with him, because here he is telling me, with relish, that without his permission to leave, I am trapped here; proving to me, yet again, that the Socialist Republic of Viet Nam is independent and powerful and not to be trifled with.

This situation is merely a new incarnation of essentially the same one that I have experienced many, many times during my two short months in Viet Nam. Adopting my humblest and most concerned smile, I ask for and receive details about this form. I protest that I would like nothing more than to follow the rules and present him with the form in question, but I never received it when I entered the country. He informs me that it was, in fact, given to me when I entered. I wrinkle my brow and speak in a conciliatory and concerned tone; after all, there is a problem here, and the two of us—myself and my friend the official—are going to work together to solve it. "What can I do if they never gave me the form?" He seems to soften just a bit, but then—remembering that he is a Vietnamese bureaucrat—hardens and says, "You get when enter, must have one for leave,"—here it comes again—"so go back Saigon get one."

Again the worried problem solver, I respond, "Well, I didn't have very much stuff, so maybe they never gave me one. But now the big problem is that if you get it when you enter the country, it will be impossible for me to get one now, even if I do go back to Saigon." Is it the merciless logic of my argument, the humility in my voice as we talk, or the fact that I intersperse the conversation with Vietnamese? Could it be that I'm not displaying the frayed temper of a typical Western plaything, nor the panic of a potential palm-greaser? Whichever, I am waved through and exit Viet Nam.

Off the Rails in Phnom Penh

Across the soccer-field sized no man's land, I enter Cambodia. Except for the glorious gate, the Cambodian side is a decidedly shabbier affair; basically a series of shacks for visa, customs, and quarantine. I wonder how many borders in the world separate such distinctly different peoples. Unlike, for example, the Thai-Cambodian, or the Vietnamese-Chinese frontiers, the border here separates not only two distinct countries, but two very distinct ethnic groups as well. The difference between the Vietnamese and Khmers is quite apparent; darker complexions, less 'oriental' features—something just a bit more mysterious in the Khmer faces. But this border within Indochina also represents the demarcation line between two of the world's greatest cultural civilizations. On the Vietnamese side is a culture heavily dominated by Chinese influence. On the Khmer side lies a culture whose roots lie deep within the Indian subcontinent.

With pleasing swiftness, I am processed through and walk on to the waiting taxis. 'Taxis' is an optimistic misnomer for these jalopies; jumping in for the ride to Phnom Penh reminds me of the high school gang piling into my friend's Duster for a road trip. Speaking Vietnamese, I arrange my passage. Four of us squeeze into the back seat of a weathered gas guzzler from the early 80s. As the taxi moves out, I am impressed by the music blaring from the ancient stereo system. Our driver has selected a tape which I can only describe as Afro-Indian style hip-hop. For the past two months in Viet Nam, my musical anthology has been limited to insipid, mainstream American fare like Michael Bolton or Mariah Carey, or sappy, Euro-pop-derivative Vietnamese love songs. In contrast, the rhythms and melodies pumping out of the taxi's stereo are vibrant and refreshing.

As we begin the drive toward Phnom Penh, I note that the road is far shabbier here than on the Vietnamese side of the border. The taxi is swerving from one side of the road to the other to avoid the potholes. Even the scenery is shabbier— long stretches of barren or haphazardly sown paddy. With the window on one side, I am sitting next to (almost on top of) a Khmer woman in her late 30s who is studying medicine in Saigon. Her English is excellent, and we chat amiably. When I note the passing landscape of sparsely populated fields, she tells me bluntly that, "Everyone is dead from Pol Pot"—including ten of her 12 siblings. A friend's statement rings in my head; "From an airplane, you can clearly see the border between Cambodia and Thailand. On the Thai side, all the fields are green, while on the Cambodian side, you see huge stretches of brown. You can see Cambodia's problems 'literally' written on the ground below you." The dust is noticeably worse on the Cambodian side, and the houses we pass also have a more rundown appearance. Oblivious, the taxi swerves its way towards Phnom Penh around potholes, motorcycles, horse-drawn or motorcycle-drawn carts, water buffalo, and other miscellaneous oncoming traffic.

We reach the Mekong, and the taxi stops to wait for the ferry crossing. We are surrounded by children and old people selling their wares; bottled water for the heat and thirst, individually wrapped towelettes for the dust, and all sorts of snacks for the munchies. I am impressed by the bananas that are mashed flat, ironed into two dimensional squares, and then rolled into cylinders. Even more impressive are the women and girls making their way through the crowds with huge platters on their heads piled high with food for sale. The platters seem rock steady as the women gracefully weave around the cars and waiting passengers selling their snacks. The day is wearing on now, and I am not eager to get back in the crowded taxi for the rest of the trip.

More rural scenes follow until we cross the bridge into Phnom Penh. As we wind our way through the urban commotion, I try to take in the atmosphere of this dirty but colorful, dusty but bustling city—really a town of small shopfronts and two or three-story apartment buildings along with a scattering of incredibly beautiful and ornate temples. Occasionally we pass a decrepit larger building that appears to have survived from the pre-communist period of the early 1970s. Even less frequently a new, modern, four-story 'skyscraper' rises from the ashes of this once graceful and charming city. The taxi driver is familiar with the Majestic Guesthouse—it is, after all, the destination of choice for those tourists who are frugal and/or courageous enough to come to Cambodia overland instead of by air. After the taxi drops me off at the guesthouse, I arrange a room and then stretch out on the bed for a nap. The room's peeling paint and modest furnishings give it a worn feel, but it is undeniably clean and comfortably large. Even in this unfamiliar setting, I soon nod off.

After a short doze and a quick shower, I begin exploring the area. The guesthouse lies off a main boulevard, and the unpaved street is a celebration of mud, trash, furrows, and fetid puddles. The dwellings and shops are mostly decaying two or three-story concrete buildings interspersed with ramshackle wooden shacks. At the intersection with another dirt road, a low pile of festering garbage serves as an unofficial traffic circle. An old woman walks by, carrying a pole balanced across her shoulder with a basket hanging off each end. I see noodles and sauces in the baskets, and am assaulted by a distinctly unpleasant fish smell.

It may not have whetted my appetite, but the slop in the baskets has reminded me that I haven't eaten since early morning, so I return to the Majestic for a meal, and also to begin my 'interviews.' I meet Fred and Samuel, two English teachers. As soon as I had decided to write about Phnom Penh, I invented a cover story to conceal that fact. I told people I was in Phnom Penh on a much-needed break from biology research on marine life in southern Vietnam's coastal waters. My story, concocted hastily during my visa run, is now delivered smoothly.

"Relaxing from research, that's a new one," says Samuel. "Everyone else comes to Cambodia for one of three reasons— guns, girls or ganja."

"You're here for at least two of them," Fred jokes with Samuel.

These quips give me an idea for the subtitle of the book I'm planning. Fred then asks me if I plan to visit Champagne (a prostitute pick-up bar). The conversation soon degenerates into a discourse about 'shagging.' This was the first time I had heard this British expression, and it didn't take long to figure out that it refers to sexual intercourse. I hope that I can successfully feign only a fleeting interest in their conversation as these two, soon joined by others who have come to eat, discuss intimate details of their hired sexual encounters. As the conversation winds down, I retire upstairs and write up my notes. Several pages of my notebook are soon filled with stories of "excellent shags" and "lousy blowjobs", "stained sheets," and "appropriate tips." When I get to the line, "I had to pay her an extra two bucks to take it up the ass," I must pause for a break. Even though I was just there, I'm still slightly thrown at the openness and explicitness with which they discussed their paid sexual escapades.

Phnom Penh's Shabby Quaintness
October 21, 1996

In my opinion, vegetarian food is the best bet for the first few meals in a new country; it is easier for the body to adjust to the new cuisine when no carcasses are involved. A friend in Viet Nam mentioned a vegetarian restaurant near the Central Market, and my mission for the day is to find it. There is a large map of Phnom Penh in the guesthouse, and I see that we are quite close to Monivong Boulevard, the capital's main north-south thoroughfare. Walking north on this main road will take me very close to the Central Market.

As I walk, I take in the scene on Monivong. On one side of the road, the head office of the Liberal Democratic Party provides evidence of open political activity. On the other side, a large and beautiful wat is evidence of indigenous artistic achievement. In this respect Cambodia is ahead of it's looming neighbor; both of these are sorely deficient in Viet Nam. Monivong itself is paved, but potholed and congested. The notion of traffic lanes is more or less meaningless, but the traffic generally does travel on the right hand side of the road. One thing I can already tell will be a prevalent theme in Phnom Penh is the air pollution. Passing me as I amble along the sidewalk is a constant stream of vehicles spewing gases and

*kicking up dust. There are hundreds of three-wheeled, envi-
ronmentally friendly pedicabs—called cyclos, but these are
outnumbered by thousands and thousands of 50 or 100cc
motor scooters sputtering and belching past.*

*Continuing on, I enter what seems to be Phnom Penh's
city center. It is a busy collection of large hotels, small shops
and travel agencies, and restaurants of all sizes. This 'downtown' is bereft of the high rises and fancy boutiques of Bangkok, or even Saigon, but it's coming along.*

*At Street 130, I turn left toward the river, which runs basi-
cally north-south and marks the eastern edge of the city. As
soon as I turn I can see the large art-deco style building that
houses the Central Market. It is a huge structure with an enormous central dome and four giant wings radiating to the north-
east, southeast, northwest, and southwest. As I scout around
the exterior, I notice a vendor carrying a platter on her head. I
can't identify her wares at first but when she takes it down to
show to prospective customers, I can see a glistening mound
of fried crickets. The sight confirms my plan to eat vegetarian.*

*I soon find the restaurant—CH Vegetarian Place. In another
example of Phnom Penh's melting pot of cultures, the restaurant is a Chinese establishment, with Taiwanese and
Singaporean backpackers seated at a couple of the tables.
Typically, for Phnom Penh, there is an added, outlandish twist.
Checking out the magazines at the tables and the decor on
the walls, I quickly realize that this place is devoted to some
kind of religious cult or sect. There is a television playing a
video tape in English with both Chinese and Vietnamese sub-
titles. The tape is describing the doctrine and achievements
and endeavors of one Supreme Master (SuMa) Ching Hai. The
Master is actually a mistress; a garishly dressed lady who
carries a broad Buddha smile and apparently performs he-
roic amounts of fundraising for charitable causes all over the
world. The video is showing SuMa Ching Hai accepting an
award in the US for organizing and financing disaster relief
in the wake of the 1993 floods in the US Midwest. She is
dressed in a gown, the centerpiece of which is a golden*

headpiece with 'rays' of cloth sweeping across her forehead. The governors of four Midwestern states are praising SuMa Ching Hai to high heaven.

After a filling but unexceptional lunch, I am eager to continue my exploration of the city by heading toward the river. The walk takes me through a mixed, dense urban setting. I pass one modern, high fashion eyeglass boutique next door to a noodle shop that looks unchanged from the 1950s. The neighborhood consists mostly of two or three-story structures, with shops on the ground level and apartments above. There are some exceptions, but very little of the gleaming glass and steel associated with big city 'downtowns.'

The river turns out to be only a leisurely ten minute stroll away. I move south along the embankment, and for the first time really appreciate the vastness of the sky. Looking eastward across the river, there are no buildings above one story. Up and down the entire length of the Mekong, there is nothing to block one's view of this big, beautiful, blue sky. Across the riverfront road are many restaurants, obviously catering to the 'rich' foreign tourists and expatriates. They have names like Riverside, Wagon Wheel, or La Taverne, without any Khmer identification at all.

The bright morning has already drifted into late afternoon. Turning west on Street 178, I return to the guesthouse. Phnom Penh has impressed me with its rustic and quaint atmosphere. The city is both shabby and relaxed, both squalid and delightful. After washing the dust off my face and hands, I lie down on the bed. I soon fall asleep to visions of potholed roads, peeling paint, and broad, slightly shy, Khmer smiles.

The Birthday of HM the King
October 31, 1996

Today is the 74th birthday of King Norodom Sihanouk. Sihanouk, like Pol Pot and Loon Nol, is one of the few Cambodian names that I had already heard of even before coming to Cambodia. Although I have yet to learn the full details,

I know that Sihanouk is a central figure in modern Cambodian history. His birthday is an official holiday, with banks and businesses closed, fireworks planned for this evening, and a festival atmosphere around the Royal Palace and the adjoining riverside area. Whether out of fealty to their semi-divine king, or as an excuse to take the day off, the Khmers take this holiday seriously.

Late morning at the Majestic, the atmosphere is also festive because there are no classes today. Those few conscientious teachers who refrain from smoking weed on workdays are smoking today. Others who do get stoned before class are smoking even more heavily than usual. A couple of groups are organizing themselves for trips to Svay Pa, the brothel village about 40 minutes outside of town. While it is common to make quick visits to brothels within the city before, after, or between English classes, Svay Pa is far enough away that men usually go only when they are free to stay for at least a couple of hours. Sunday is the usual Svay Pa day, but the King's birthday offers another perfect opportunity.

As usual, I am soaking up the activity and atmosphere around me. While calling a waiter over to take my order, I am interrupted by Reiner. He and I have chatted a couple of times before at the Majestic. A budding entrepreneur, Reiner is a great big dynamo of a human being. He is from Britain, born of a Kenyan mother and a German father. Reiner tells me he is heading to Bhase's and asks me if I would like to join him. When I show my ignorance, he pounces on the opportunity to enlighten me about this place. "It's a Tamil Indian restaurant near the Central Market. It's brilliant," he declares enthusiastically.

We hop on one moto together, which is somewhat uncomfortable given Reiner's size. After a short and awkward ride, we arrive at the restaurant. It is on the same road as the Central Market, but closer to the river. I immediately take a liking to the restaurant's sign. Along with the name of the place, it has a picture of a fork and a spoon given human faces. The thing is, they are not happily encouraging guests to eat and spend more money, a la Ronald McDonald; no,

16

these utensils have very serious and thoughtful, almost sinister expressions.

Inside is a mid-sized Phnom Penh restaurant, cozy by American standards. I immediately see that most of the customers are Indians—more specifically, I presume, Tamils. The system that Reiner has described for dining here is still unclear to me, and he snaps impatiently when I ask for a menu. When the waitress comes out to take our order, I am still floundering. Reiner takes matters into his own hands and orders; "Two vegetable meals on plates with rice."

With that crisis out of the way, I now have a chance to observe our fellow diners. There is definitely a sense of community here. The owner of the place seems to know everyone by name, and chats with each of the customers in turn. They shout over the din of a TV which is showing Indian music videos at maximum volume. Everyone in the place is eating with their hands—plunging their fingers into the rice and mixing it with whatever else constitutes the main dish, and then scooping it indelicately into their mouths. The rice many of these guys are handling does not sit on plates, but rather what look like green placemats—actually banana leaves; not only is this eco-friendly, it also saves on the washing up.

Like so many other places in Phnom Penh, this one has its own bizarre twist. Reiner smiles and nods towards a gentleman in the corner speaking earnestly, but with good humor, to a group of younger men who are all listening intently.

"Last month," Reiner begins to explain, "the Phnom Penh Post ran a couple of articles about the Tigers buying SAM missiles and other weaponry in Cambodia from corrupt generals and the KR."

I presume correctly that "Tigers" refers to the Tamil Tigers, the separatist guerrilla army fighting for a Tamil homeland in northern Sri Lanka. Reiner is keen to let me know that KR is the Phnom Penh shorthand for Khmer Rouge, and that SAM refers to surface-to-air missiles. I am already aware of these abbreviations but I indulge him as he continues enthusiastically; "They talk about the main organizer of the Tamil Tigers in Phnom Penh; that man we just nodded to, that's him."

17

Reiner laughs at my sudden unease. "Don't worry about it. It's completely casual to eat here, but don't show too much interest if two people are having a quiet, serious discussion."

I have a new appreciation for the sense of community I find here, but my musings are interrupted by the food. We are handed two metal plates and one large platter heaped with rice. The vegetables come next in a serving contraption which is completely new to me; four deep bowls, about seven inches tall and three inches in diameter welded together with a handle. Each day, Reiner explains, the four bowls of this contraption are filled with four different vegetable dishes. We can take as much of each dish as we like and eat it with the rice on the platter between us. One thing makes me hesitate as I eat, though. The four-bowl ensemble was brought to us from the table of another, finger-licking, customer. After years of having restaurant food brought to me directly from the kitchen, it takes a moment of adjustment to have my lunch come from the table of another patron. Setting aside my reservations, I dive in, using silverware. The vegetables are simply delicious.

Conversation with Reiner is a bit one-sided, but hardly boring. He tells me about his business plans, his opinions on the difficulty of working with Khmers, and the impossibility of trusting the Vietnamese. The conviction with which he speaks fills in any gaps in his logic. The conversation continues until we have thoroughly engorged ourselves on the food. Reiner and I wind down our lunch, and I am grateful that he brought me here.

After a post-lunch rest back at the guesthouse, I decide to explore more of the city on this auspicious holiday. I rent a bicycle in order to take a relaxing afternoon ride around town. Such is the decadence of life at the Majestic that one of the residents was very sincerely impressed with my plan. What to me is a simple afternoon's physical recreation is to him an "ambitious project." I chuckle to myself at how, curled up in the guesthouse hammock smoking a joint, he watched the sun begin to go down and said, "Fuck it, I just had to do one thing today. Just one. All I wanted to do was bring my clothes to the laundry, and now it's closed. Cambodia is the only place where your 'to do' list can have only one item, and you still don't get around to it."

Although I still cannot classify it as an "ambitious project," my ride is not entirely leisurely either. Phnom Penh's dirt roads, and the potholes and sandbars on its paved roads, make for hard riding. Still, the urban scenes are worth the effort. My ride takes me past Phnom Penh's concrete apartment houses and wooden shack squatter settlements, past dilapidated schools and workshops that are closed for the holiday, and past freshly painted brothels and restaurants that are doing a brisk business.

All too soon, the sky begins to darken, indicating the end to my ride. My route back to the guesthouse will take me along the river past the Royal Palace. As I approach the palace, the opulent beauty of it takes my breath away. The first thing I notice is not even the palace itself, but rather the row of lamp-posts on the side of the street opposite the royal compound and closer to the river. Each lamppost has a flower-shaped light display roughly two yards high and one yard in diam-eter at the widest point. It is visually stunning, especially once I turn the corner and see 30 or 40 of them lining the avenue.

Soon I am in full view of the palace itself, and am stunned yet again. The palace is partly obscured by a protective wall running 400 meters on this side alone—the top of which is decorated with sensually curved merlons (the alternating walled and open sections of a castle battlement) stylized in the shape of the leaves of the sacred bo tree; much more ap-pealing than the square merlons of European castles. The entire length of this wall is decorated with light bulbs strung to follow the curves of each merlon. The resulting uninter-rupted chain of light is a visual delight.

Riding on, I come to the Chan Chaya Pavilion; an impos-ing structure in its own right. This is basically an elaborate gazebo constructed with gilded supports and beams. The roof is terraced, with orange and green tiles, and at each corner of each of the terraces, jovia flare proudly into the sky. The jovia is a decorative element of Khmer architecture—adopted and *made famous by the Thais—which can best be described as a stylized elephant trunk, raised and trumpeting triumphantly into the air. The* jovias *actually represent the tails of the* naga *which resides on the roof and protects the structure.*

The Chan Chaya Pavilion is dominated by a huge light display almost as tall as the 75-foot-high structure itself. This is the royal emblem—sculpted in light and blazing its glory along the road and on down to the river. My eyes are beguiled by the spectacle before me, and I am not paying attention to the road. Some subconscious order tells me that I should look ahead. I follow this command and am surprised by an elephant lumbering down the road in front of, and directly toward me. Certain that I would emerge the loser in a head-on collision, I swerve. I miss the elephant but come unnervingly close to a passing motorcycle.

"Always tripping" indeed. I turn the corner to head back to the guesthouse and laugh to myself thinking about being back in the US filing a police report concerning my incident with the elephant; "But you see, officer, it wasn't my fault, the elephant was coming down the wrong side of the road."

History

"It's not too difficult to imagine
in fifty years Cambodia won't
even exist at all. It'll just be
swallowed completely by
Thailand and Viet Nam."

Anyone looking for fascinating tales or ludicrous anecdotes will find a gold mine in Cambodia's recent history and current government. Social disorder and political chaos—the results of decades of civil war and misgovernment—were all around me during my time in Phnom Penh. For example, although patently illegal, prostitution is practiced openly and conspicuously. While the majority of Cambodians labor in abject poverty, government officials with nominal salaries of $16 a month drive $50,000 cars. For the past 27 years, Khmers have demonstrated an astonishing willingness to murder each other. A glance at the newspapers, with the two (two!) Prime Ministers accusing each other of being Vietnamese and Khmer Rouge puppets (respectively), provides more questions than answers. In light of all this, one wonders what warped historical process could have created a country in such disarray.

A teacher named Joe is my primary tour guide through recent Cambodian history. Joe is a tall, intelligent, thoughtful New Zealander who lived in Viet Nam in 1993, and has been in Cambodia since 1994. Joe avoids the drugs and brotheling which attract so many of his friends, but he does take girls home from Champagne if he thinks there is a chance of developing a relationship. He has been involved with progres-

21

sive causes in New Zealand for years, and he came to Asia to see firsthand such issues as social development, labor relations, economic development, and political repression. Joe has found more than he bargained for in Cambodia. Besides teaching English, he spends his time learning Khmer and studying Cambodian history. He is perspicacious and well-read, and freely acknowledges his own biases. We sometimes disagree with each other, but I always value our discussions.

Most regulars at the Majestic are neither interested in, nor knowledgeable about, the history of their adopted country. But among the Majestic patrons are also teachers like Joe, journalists, NGO workers, and others who are very aware of current and historical events. Over many conversations with them, and through newspaper articles and books on the subject, I begin to unravel the tangle of Cambodian politics. While the notes I took could easily develop into a separate book, I was able to distill all of it into a necessarily incomplete summary of recent Cambodian history—not only interesting in its own right, but also crucial to any understanding of Cambodia today.

The most glorious era of Khmer history was from the tenth to fifteenth centuries, when the Angkor kings ruled an empire that stretched over most of Southeast Asia. They used their wealth to build fantastic monuments—such as the justifiably famous Angkor Wat—and they developed a cultural tradition that still thrives in Cambodia, Thailand, and Laos today. For recent Cambodian history, however, we can use 1953 as a starting point. In that year, Prince Norodom Sihanouk[1] negotiated independence from the French, who were bogged down in the war in Viet Nam. Sihanouk was very popular and dominated Cambodian politics until 1970. Although hardly paradise, Cambodia in the 1950s and most of the 1960s was largely content, peaceful and prosperous. In fact, a delegation from newly-independent Singapore showed up in 1965 to learn how to run a successful country.

---

[1] Now *King* Sihanouk. Between 1965 and 1993 he relinquished the title King in order to participate directly in politics. The title was restored in 1993.

Trouble began in the late 1960s with the ongoing war in Viet Nam. The Communists were using neutral Cambodia as a base and sanctuary to attack South Viet Nam, and the US retaliated—first in the form of 'secret' bombings, and then with invasions. Sihanouk tried to keep Cambodia out of the war, but it was difficult because first the Communists, then the Americans were violating Cambodian neutrality. Sihanouk did not want to take too strong a stand against the Vietnamese. Firstly, he reasoned, very astutely, that while the Americans would leave just like the French had, Viet Nam and Cambodia would always be neighbors. Secondly, the Chinese were paying a commission for transporting supplies to the Viet Cong through Cambodia, so Sihanouk's government was getting its hands on a lot of cash and weaponry.

This situation continued until March 1970, when pro-American, anti-Communist elements in Sihanouk's government led by General Loon Nol staged a parliamentary coup and deposed the prince from office while he was out of the country. Loon Nol renamed the country the Khmer Republic and looked to the United States for massive backing to fund the subsequent fight against the Khmer Communists and their Vietnamese allies. Prince Sihanouk sought to regain power from Loon Nol, so he allied himself with the Communists—whom the world would come to know as the barbaric Khmer Rouge—under Pol Pot. From 1970 to 1975 they fought a terrible civil war. On one side were the Khmer Rouge, who had been in the jungle for years and now had the prestige of the Prince behind them. On the other side was the Khmer Republic, an increasingly corrupt, incompetent, and autocratic government almost completely bankrolled by the US Treasury. The Americans also contributed directly to the war effort through a merciless bombing campaign—dropping 50% more tonnage on rural Cambodia in 1973 than on all of Japan during the entire Second World War. In the end, the Khmer Republic was doomed, primarily because of the unbelievable corruption and incompetence of its leaders.

One of the many charges of outrageous Khmer Republican corruption was revealed in documents graciously shown to me by Dr. Max Henn, whose Western Union Finance Company in Vientiane served as a message and intelligence center for the region between 1965 and 1976. His documents show that key Khmer Republican leaders were part owners of charter air services which the Americans contracted to airlift supplies to Phnom Penh as it fell under siege from the Khmer Rouge in late 1974 and early 1975. Thus, central figures in the Loon Nol regime had a direct financial interest in not breaking the siege that was choking their own government and capital city. This siege, of course, destroyed the front-line morale of Loon Nol's soldiers, and created miserable conditions for the hundreds of thousands of refugees who came to Phnom Penh to escape the US bombing in the countryside.

A more serious charge, also revealed in Dr. Henn's files, is reported to the general public for the first time ever in this book. It is common knowledge that attempts were made to end the civil war by bringing together pro-Sihanouk leaders in the Khmer Rouge-Sihanouk alliance, and moderate elements in the Khmer Republican leadership. The conventional wisdom is that the 'secret' effort fell through only after it was prematurely leaked to the world press by third country diplomats involved. However, documents in Dr. Henn's possession prove that Sihanouk, who was (and still is) incensed at his ignominious deposition from power in 1970, refused to countenance any negotiations whatsoever. Dr. Henn had been playing a central role in establishing contacts between the two sides. This ended when a telegram, delivered to Dr. Henn from the Prince's envoy, explained that Sihanouk, ". . . does not accept any compromise or negotiations with the Lon Nol clique."

While it is unclear whether a coalition government could ever have formed, Dr. Henn's documents raise disturbing questions. Although Sihanouk had serious misgivings about his Khmer Rouge allies, he refused to explore any other solution but their victory. Given the disastrous civil war raging at the time, and the brutal reign of madness that resulted after the Khmer Rouge took power, the charge that Sihanouk let his personal pique at being deposed keep him from exploring a way to prevent the tragedies which haunt Cambodia to this day is a dark stain on any assessment of this Cambodian leader.

Finally, on 17th April 1975, Phnom Penh fell to the Khmer Rouge. The tragic history of Cambodia from 1975 to 1979 is well known, and is documented in detail in many other publications. It is also well represented in the movie *The Killing Fields*. Pol Pot's Khmer Rouge put Sihanouk under house arrest and then turned Cambodia into an agrarian 'concentration camp' with absolutely no tolerance for dissent from the Party line. An arbitrary and merciless slaughter of 'undesirable' sections of the population began immediately. Reliable statistics are unavailable, but a reasonable estimate is that between one and two million people (of a population of about seven million) died from starvation, disease, overwork, or execution during the Khmer Rouge genocide. Hardest hit were professionals; teachers, doctors, skilled workers, monks, and artists—essentially all the people that contemporary Cambodia desperately needs in order to rebuild its shattered economy, society, and culture.

The key to understanding contemporary Cambodian politics is that the Khmer Rouge turned on their Vietnamese Communist allies and began launching border raids and massacring Vietnamese civilians (many of them ethnic Khmers) on the Vietnamese side of the border. There has long been historic animosity between the Vietnamese and the Khmers. Most of southern Viet Nam was once Khmer territory. The Khmers consider the Vietnamese devious swindlers, and the Vietnamese consider the Khmers disorganized primitives. The problem is that, in a sense, both views are correct. The Khmer Rouge were trying to reconquer land which Viet Nam annexed from Cambodia in 1623. Whether or not they were justified, it was ludicrous to attempt it by force. Pol Pot's leadership also began purging cadres they felt were too pro-Vietnamese, not revolutionary enough, or who posed a threat to Pol Pot's power. In light of the purges, a number of cadres, afraid for their lives, fled to Viet Nam. There they were organized by the Vietnamese into an alternative Cambodian government.

In December 1978, after continuing Khmer Rouge provocations, the Vietnamese launched a full-scale invasion—supposedly only to "assist" these former Khmer Rouge who had fled to Viet Nam. The Vietnamese troops were welcomed as liberators at first, because anything was better than life under the Khmer Rouge. The invading troops very quickly drove the Khmer Rouge into the jungle and put the defectors in power. One of the men they installed was Hun Sen, who is, at the time of writing, Second Prime Minister.

From 1979 to 1989, Vietnamese troops and the Hun Sen forces fought a civil war against an alliance calling for the withdrawal of Vietnamese troops from Cambodia. The resistance consisted of the Khmer Rouge, the Royalists (FUNCINPEC—an acronym of the French for National United Front for an Independent, Neutral, Peaceful and Co-Operative Cambodia), and a third Buddhist, anti-Communist faction. Hun Sen and the Vietnamese were backed by the Soviets, and the resistance was supported by ASEAN, the US, and China. Consider the political choice of a Cambodian during this era; on one side, he or she could support a government installed and maintained by the occupation forces of Viet Nam—a country with a long history of subjugating, colonizing, and annexing Khmer lands. On the other side, he or she could support a resistance alliance dominated by the Khmer Rouge—responsible for the deaths of a huge proportion of the country's population.

Under US and Chinese pressure, the Vietnamese agreed to withdraw their troops in 1989, and in 1991 the warring factions signed the Paris Peace Accords. These Accords ended the civil war and called for power sharing among the four factions to be followed by an election—supervised by the United Nations Transitional Authority in Cambodia (UNTAC)—and the formation of a new government based on the election results. After the truce, power was theoretically held by all four factions, who together comprised the Supreme National Council. But in fact, the apparatus of the state was still in the hands of the Hun Sen Communists, who by now had renounced Communism and become the Cambodian People's Party (CPP). The Peace Accords disintegrated—with the CPP abusing the police and state-controlled media to rig the election, the Khmer Rouge returning to the jungles to fight, and the UN personnel doing as much drinking and whoring as their bloated $145 *daily* allowances would allow.

The elections were held in July 1993. FUNCINPEC, the Royalists led by the King's son, Prince Norodom Ranaridh, won a plurality. Together with the Buddhist anti-Communists, they had a majority. Still, the CPP refused to relinquish power. Because they, the losers of the elections, controlled most of the newly integrated army, the only way to truly enforce the results would have been for all the UN peacekeepers to leave the brothels and bars and go into the streets to fight. Eventually Sihanouk and the UN brokered a compromise between Hun Sen and Ranaridh; the two would serve as co-Prime Ministers, and authority over the various ministries would be split between the parties. The compromise began well. However, over the past four years, Hun Sen has used his military and financial advantages along with his superior skills in political maneuvering—with Machiavellian ruthlessness—in order to intimidate, kill, co-opt, or exile many of those who oppose him. So, at the time I began learning about Cambodian politics, the situation was thus; a Mafia-like former Communist slowly eroding the power base of a popularly elected but ineffective Prince.

But Cambodian politics do not remain stable for long. Very soon after I first arrived in Cambodia, a process began that will have dramatic implications for the country. The decline of the Khmer Rouge as a Communist guerrilla opposition has been a long, drawn-out process that has yet to end completely. But the conclusion is in sight—and it offers the likelihood that, for the first time in over three decades, Cambodia could be free from any large-scale civil war.

Just as I arrived in Cambodia came the first reports of a major split between the two main Khmer Rouge (KR) encampments—one in the north, centered around Anlong Veng, the other in the northwest, centered around Pailin. By November, the entirety of the Pailin forces left the control of the KR central command and joined the government. This effectively halved the number of KR guerrillas, as well as removed from KR control Pailin's lucrative gem trade—estimated to have brought in as much as $10 million per month to the faction. Although, on paper, fully integrated into the Royal Government of Cambodia, the former KR in Pailin in fact maintain a high degree of autonomy—more or less directing their own affairs with little input from Phnom Penh.

Attention then turned to the remaining Khmer Rouge under Pol Pot in Anlong Veng. In early 1997, talks began in earnest between representatives of FUNCINPEC and Anlong Veng. FUNCINPEC's stated goal was to end the war by enlisting the Anlong Veng guerrillas to defect to the government—as had the Pailin KR. But the reality was more complex. The FUNCINPEC strategists envisioned that the KR structures would remain largely intact, again like Pailin, but that they would be closely aligned with FUNCINPEC in its struggle against the CPP.

Two key individuals had a lot to lose from this strategy, and both took action against it. Although we may never know for certain, observers presume that a power struggle ensued in Anlong Veng over the question of rehabilitation into the legitimate national political fold. The leader of the Pailin KR, Ieng Sary—second in command for much of the DK (Democratic Kampuchea—the KR government) period, and a man with much blood on his hands—was painfully granted amnesty in order to expedite an end to the fighting. After much bitter argument, Cambodia in effect exchanged justice for peace. It was fairly well established that Pol Pot, the man most closely identified with the horrors of the DK regime, would never be given a similar deal—neither by Cambodia, nor by the international community.

Thus, Pol Pot must have realized that integration with the government would leave him powerless, at best. On June 9, 1997, he began what was fated to be the last of his many internal Party purges by killing a high ranking associate and

his family. The murders plunged Anlong Veng into chaos. After ten days of confusion came the dramatic announcement
on KR radio that Pol Pot had been arrested and imprisoned
for treason.

With Pol Pot finally deposed, the FUNCINPEC-Anlong Veng
negotiations continued. By July 4, 1997, they had reached a
dramatic agreement; the KR would end their war against the
government and become a legitimate political faction.

It was at this stage that the other key player threatened by
the negotiations took action. For a decade, Hun Sen had fought
against an armed resistance made up of the KR and
FUNCINPEC alliance. He could not sit idly by as this alliance
was resurrected in the political arena. Although he could not
eliminate the KR, he could get rid of FUNCINPEC. On July 5th
and 6th, Hun Sen's soldiers launched attacks which threw the
entire FUNCINPEC organization into disarray, and forced First
Prime Minister, Prince Ranaridh to flee the country (he had
actually been warned of the attacks and departed beforehand).
While the coup made headlines, it merely consolidated a situation which had been in effect long before. The main difference was that, whereas before the coup, FUNCINPEC could
offer muffled and feeble resistance to Hun Sen's control, now
he wielded almost absolute power.

Even with the coup in the foreground, the protracted de-
mise of the KR continued. The headline-grabbing show trial
of Pol Pot in August 1997 was further evidence that the KR
was still engaged in the uphill (many would say quixotic) battle to shed the image of their infamous past. A more dramatic
break came in March of 1998. Mirroring Pailin's split 18 months
earlier, entire divisions of the Anlong Veng KR mutinied
against Ta Mok, the man who succeeded Pol Pot, and joined
the government. At a stroke, KR forces were reduced to a few
hundred men, and vast areas of KR territory were brought
under government control. The death of Pol Pot, announced
shortly after the mutinies, seemed a perfect metaphor; this
ultra-nationalist movement which he led, and which had
brought untold suffering to the nation, might soon be as dead
as its longtime leader. Although political and random violence

are likely to remain well into Cambodia's future, at the time of writing, Cambodia looked set to enjoy, for the first time in 30 years, an end to large-scale civil war.

Beneath this brief sketch lurks a dizzying array of violence, corruption, intrigue, and sheer inanity. The UNTAC period alone offers political satirists a lifetime worth of material. A few UNTAC veterans are still around, and their stories are so incredible that they could only come from a UN operation. One man, whose tenure in Cambodia spanned from UNTAC until the July 1997 coup, tells me about the period; "UNTAC personnel were given a hundred and forty-five dollars *a day* for living expenses—in a country where the average income is about a hundred and twenty a year. The worst were the Bulgarians, or as they were known, the 'Vulgarians.' Even with their huge allowances, they had a habit of bringing whores to the hotel and then not paying them in the morning. The managers used to get really pissed off with having to deal with these angry taxi-girls. I heard that to fill its UNTAC quota at the beginning, the Bulgarians just took people out of the jails, thinking it would be a dangerous assignment. When they found out what a piece of cake UNTAC was, the first lot were sent home and replaced with others. The new ones were just as bad, but they had better connections. There are stories like one drunk 'Vulgarian' pissing on a beggar in the middle of the street.

"When you think about it, the whole enterprise was ludicrous. UNTAC came here to establish democracy and human rights and root out corruption in the government, right? And to do that, they used policemen from Nigeria, Indonesia, and all these other corruption-free bastions of democracy and human rights. Not only that, but it was against UNTAC policy to test personnel for HIV. So, you had these whore-crazy Indians and Africans fanning out into the far corners of the country and bringing AIDS to every village in Cambodia. It's like some kind of missionary project gone mad. There was one UNTAC guy who was treated for VD something like fifty times. It got so bad that headquarters issued a directive asking UNTAC personnel to stop parking the UN vehicles in front of brothels all the time. Even as peacekeepers, the UNTAC personnel couldn't keep themselves under control. There were so many brawls at Champagne between the Americans and French, eventually the bar just banned all American servicemen.

"It makes me angry when people talk about spending three billion *on* Cambodia. It was actually three billion *through* Cambodia—but most of that went to the UNTAC guys. You know, many of the countries who sent personnel actually took a direct cut of their money. And then, when push came to shove and the CPP refused to accept that they lost, UNTAC didn't lift a damn finger to enforce the results. So they came up with this 'compromise.' Great! The losers retained power over the winners. They always talk about UNTAC as the UN's greatest success. What utter bullshit."

That the elections passed muster as "free and fair" makes sense only in the perverse context of Cambodia. Says one UNTAC veteran; "The CPP pulled every trick they could to win the election. Our employees translated some of the stuff they broadcast over the radio. One broadcast said that the ballot wasn't really secret because spy satellites could look through the roofs of the polling stations and see who voted for whom. And they said that people who voted against the CPP would have to worry about 'indignant masses avenging their betrayal of the people.'"

He relates another anecdote; "There was this woman leader in an ethnic Vietnamese village. She was saying that the CPP and the KR would always be fighting—so if Ranaridh won, that would be the best chance for peace, and then the Vietnamese wouldn't have to worry about being massacred by the KR. She disappeared. About a week later the police dumped her body in the middle of the village so everyone could see she'd been tortured and killed for working against the CPP. There was a lot of this. But even with all the evidence of killing and intimidation [of opposition party workers], UNTAC didn't crack down on the CPP because they didn't want to upset their big 'success' in Cambodia. Finally, they declared it all [the election] 'free and fair enough.' It was pathetic."

Even given the irrationality of the operation that created the current government, some of the antics of Cambodia's politicians still defy belief. For example, a visiting Bangkok-based journalist jokingly tells me of Hun Sen's "devotion to freedom of speech." He explains how last year a newspaper that was outspoken in its opposition to the government was ransacked by a gang of thugs. The presses were destroyed and the building gutted. They were from Hun Sen's 'model development village' and were directed by commanders with walkie-talkies. Still, Hun Sen claimed that he had nothing to do with it. He claimed that it was a spontaneous reaction on the part of people who were angry at the "lies" being printed by the newspaper. In retrospect, however, he felt that the attack was not such a bad idea, even though, of course, he had nothing at all to do with it.

The journalist concludes this story with bitter irony; "After all, Cambodia is a democracy and democracy means freedom of speech. The people rampaging through the newspaper's offices were just exercising their freedom of speech. In fact, Hun Sen said he is such a great defender of civil liberties that if a spontaneous gathering wants to ransack another opposition newspaper, he'll transport them using his own trucks."

"Here's another one," the journalist continues. "Hun Sen engineered a split in the BLDP [Buddhist Liberal Democratic Party]. Apparently he bribed and intimidated the number two man, Ieng Mouly, to try and take over. The old leader, Son Sann, refused to let Mouly betray the party's principles for money. He scheduled a sort of party congress to decide what to do. Hun Sen predicted—he didn't threaten, he just predicted—there might be a grenade attack on the meeting. He wouldn't have anything to do with it, of course, he just had an inkling it would happen. And you know what? He was right. There was a grenade attack and sixteen people who refused to follow Ieng Mouly over to Hun Sen's side were killed. And of course, Hun Sen wasn't involved at all."

In the mental model I develop to understand Cambodian politics, violence serves as the means to obtain and maintain power—and power as the means to profit from corruption. It is easy to find other examples proving that violence is a common theme in Cambodian politics. A photographer shows me a picture that all-too-perfectly captures the tragic results of political violence. In the photograph, a frail seven or eight-year-old boy is wearing the long white robe and headscarf of Cambodian mourning, and his hands are rubbing the tears from his eyes. Dwarfing the boy's small frame is a clear plastic riot shield with the word POLICE emblazoned in yellow across it. The boy is standing right up against the shield, weeping.

The photographer relates the story behind the picture; "In May '96, a newspaper editor called Thun Bun Ly was assassinated. His paper had been openly critical of Hun Sen. They'd printed stuff about his 'dictatorship of money and violence.' As if proving him right, Hun Sen had him killed. The funeral turned into an anti-government protest when the police prevented them from marching past the National Assembly."

Another reporter explains that, "Bun Ly was the fourth journalist killed since the election. In the election itself, hundreds of FUNCINPEC and BLDP candidates and workers were killed, beaten, tortured, or targeted for intimidation."

Even if violence is not actually used, the threat of violence is a constant reality. As one Khmer human rights worker put it; "We try to do our jobs well, but it's difficult. We know how easy it is for someone to follow us home from the office and beat or kill us. We know how easily someone could toss a grenade into our office." The March 30 grenade attack on peaceful demonstrators (described in detail in Chapter 5) is yet another example of how easily the threat of political violence becomes a reality.

The tales of corruption which flow from power are every bit as incredible as the tales of violence which lead to power. One long-term resident tells us a rumor he's heard, "from a source who's reliable, but not conclusive." The story is certainly believable. "The money we use was printed in France. Whoever was in charge of hiring the printer told the French company they'd get the contract on the condition they printed up an extra set of notes off the record. So, say the contract's for a million of the ten-thousand-*riel* notes. The company prints and ships a million notes to the National Bank of Cambodia. They also secretly deliver a hundred thousand of the ten-thousand-*riel* notes to these officials. They bring the notes to Cambodia in suitcases. It's brilliant. They created perfect counterfeits of their own money. Of course, that's what countries at war do to each other to sabotage the enemy's economy. And these Finance Ministry guys did it to their own country just so they'd have some pocket money."

Better documented is the widely acknowledged assertion that Hun Sen's "bodyguard"—in reality a 1,500-man private army—is financed by multimillionaire Theng Boon Ma, who happens to be on a US DEA blacklist because of his reputed drug smuggling. The obvious conclusion is that Theng Boon Ma, a Sino-Khmer, pays off Hun Sen in exchange for permission to rake in millions of dollars smuggling drugs through Cambodia. Even United States institutions are not immune from Cambodian corruption. Mr. Boon Ma, along with his patron Hun Sen, was even awarded an honorary doctorate from Iowa Wesleyan University. This was arranged through the intermediation of an Indonesian-born businessman wanted in the US for questioning in connection with donations to the Democratic Party. In January of 1998, Iowa Wesleyan rescinded its doctorate when the trustees learned of Mr. Boon Ma's more questionable contributions to human welfare.

Another close associate of Hun Sen also seems to be involved in the drug trade. Two journalists with long experience in Cambodia named Henry and Jake provide the details. Henry begins; "They found six tons of marijuana inside a rubber shipment for Sri Lanka, and this rubber belongs to Mong Ret Thy, one of Hun Sen's drug cronies. This guy also gets the contracts to build 'Hun Sen schools' all over the country. Then, get this typical Cambodian logic; CPP police arrested the FUNCINPEC customs guys for 'falsifying documents.' They said they'd used forged papers to frame Mong Ret Thy. But they were his anyway. Everyone knew that. Then, Hun Sen says that anyone who wanted to arrest Mong Ret Thy had better 'wear a steel helmet.' For the next few weeks, there was always a truckload of CPP soldiers parked outside Mong Ret Thy's office.

"Mong Ret Thy is Cambodia's biggest rubber exporter. Because his plantations are more efficient? Not exactly. Everyone has to pay an export tax of ten percent on rubber. Everyone except Mong Ret Thy. So, because he doesn't pay any taxes, he can undercut everyone else's price. And of course, anyone who questions the wisdom of that tax exemption had better wear a steel helmet."

Jake laughs. "That's a good name for it. The 'steel helmet' tax exemption." He continues; "So you see, Hun Sen has the power to give favors to businessmen at the expense of the national treasury. These guys then give him part of the money they save. He takes that money, which should be in the government budget, and uses it to build schools in his own name. So, he gets the credit with the government's money. And he also uses it to bribe opposition members to betray their parties and ally with him. I heard one rumor that Ieng Mouly [who split the Buddhist Liberal Democratic Party and aligned himself with Hun Sen] got over one and a half million dollars deposited in a Swiss account. There're also a lot of accusations that the CPP's been selling off land that officially belongs to the state, and putting the money in Party coffers. This was especially true when they had full run of the place in the run-up to the elections."

Another use for political money comes to light when Joe reads us an article from the September 15–30, 1996 issue of the bi-weekly Phnom Penh Post. He begins reading;

> Shifting allegiances within Cambodia's local press have exposed political patronage, corruption, and extortion to a level which insiders describe as "unprecedented" and "out of control." According to several industry sources, both major parties are offering large sums of money to Khmer editors and journalists in order to buy favorable coverage and boost their propaganda apparatus in the run up to the elections. At least two former "opposition" papers have changed their editorial line in recent weeks. In

its September 23 edition, Wat Phnom—previously associated with the Khmer Nation Party (KNP) and highly critical of government corruption—ran a stinging attack on KNP leader Sam Rainsy. "Sam Rainsy is not a democrat . . . [He] is a neo-Nazi . . . " the front page story read before going on to assert that the KNP was divided in a five way internal split being engineered by FUNCINPEC.

Joe interrupts himself; "OK, Sam Rainsy may be a publicity-seeking rabble rouser, or an anti-development activist, but a neo-Nazi, come on. And it's classic for them to accuse FUNCINPEC of organizing a split within the party. Engineering splits in opposition parties is one of the CPP's favorite tactics. You can always tell what they're up to by listening to what they accuse others of doing." Joe continues reading to us;

An editorial piece which recently appeared in Sereypheap Thmei—previously edited by a ranking KNP member, also has industry insiders perplexed. The paper ran a comment piece which praised Hun Sen as "the most outstanding figure within the CPP's leadership." One opposition editor, who requested anonymity, claimed both papers had ". . . sold out. The current editor was always urging the former editor to abandon the KNP and align with the CPP because they have more money. When the former editor died of tuberculosis, the new editor went to the CPP, who gave him $30,000."

According to Tath Lyhok, co-President of the Khmer Journalists Association, the problems of corruption, patronage and blackmail have their roots in both financial and moral bankruptcy. "Before Lon Nol, Khmers were very moral people. After the war and genocide, morality is very low—people will do anything to earn money. When I was young, I was helped by strong family values, but today there are many hypocrites. It is a very big worry for the free press. The purpose of journalists is to attack corruption, but if a newspaper is corrupt, how can it fight corruption?

Joe looks up, disgusted, "It just goes on and on about all the ways newspapers sell influence to get money from the parties. They also talk about how they blackmail people with unfavorable articles and then don't print the articles if they get bought off, and how advertisers are afraid to be associated with anti-government newspapers."

Later, a journalist working over dinner at the Majestic shows me the text of an article he is submitting for the next day's paper. It too shows the extent to which corruption is rooted at all levels of Cambodian life.

Hundreds of police surrounded local high schools to prevent the widespread cheating that consistently accompanies the annual year-end exams. Friends and family members of the students were seen throwing rocks with the answers to questions wrapped around them through the windows, while others bribed teachers and policemen not to interfere. The Minister of Education conceded that even if the police were able to prevent on-site cheating, they would not be able to prevent cheating by students who purchased the tests and answers from teachers in the days leading up to the exams. The Minister also used the occasion to point out other problems in the education system. These included teachers who cannot enforce discipline against the children of wealthy or powerful parents for fear of physical reprisal. He also mentioned that the very idea of earning a diploma was in danger, as diplomas were easy to purchase from corrupt school administrators.

As I learn more about the workings of Cambodia's government, especially Hun Sen and his Cambodian People's Party, I modify my model somewhat. Power, it seems, is often an end in itself, with corruption just a lucrative by-product. A journalist reminds me of the Khmer Rouge roots of today's CPP. "Remember, the CPP is basically Khmer Rouge in their understanding of power; once obtained, it's to be used ruthlessly in pursuit of greater power. What's most tragic is that this is always at the expense of the country."

One relative newcomer says, "There doesn't even seem to be a sense of 'Well, this is bad for the country, but I really need the money to pay for mother's operation so I'll sell out.' I mean, it's just completely unprincipled. It's not even misguided patriotism. It's pure greed, regardless of the consequences for Cambodia."

Dan, a longtime teacher married to a Khmer woman, says, "You've pretty much hit the nail on the head. Sam Rainsy is about the only figure that could ever say, 'This is bad for Cambodia, and so even though it benefits me personally, I won't agree to it. For everyone else, what's good or bad for Cambodia doesn't even enter into it."

"Son Sann," interrupts another well-informed participant.

"OK, so Sam Rainsy and Son Sann. Everyone else is out for money and power, and fuck the country and its people."

A journalist who has studied the whole of Khmer history shows how deeply rooted this ethos is. "Hun Sen basically sold out his country to the Vietnamese; they get to occupy Cambodia and he gets to rule under their thumb. I'll bet Ranaridh would do the same with the Thais if they were interested. And the Khmer Rouge have been selling Cambodia's timber and gems to the Thais for years. Did you know that rice production actually went up during Pol Pot's regime? Sure, but they sold it all to China to buy weapons, so the people starved."

He paints a very bleak picture of how selling out the country for personal power is a pattern throughout Khmer history; a major reason why the Khmer empire kept shrinking. At each succession, one contender for the throne would seek help from Viet Nam, and another from Siam. Whoever won would have to give concessions to his benefactors. Then, the defeated brother or cousin would raise more support from the other sponsor and seize the crown, thus losing more of Cambodia's independence in the process. Thus, a simplified view of Cambodian history is one of factions selling out slices of sovereignty for power over other Khmers.

"Power is the ultimate goal," he continues. "Money is only used to buy power. I mean, you've got some guy with his tinted-windowed Landcruiser driving up to the nightclub, and he's got his bodyguards with guns and handcuffs, and he can have any girl in the nightclub because he's got the cash to buy them. That right there is the pinnacle of Khmer society. It doesn't matter if he got that money by selling children to European pedophile rings. He's got power, and that's all that counts."

One journalist with experience in China makes this comparison; "The Chinese are only interested in making money, but even the *nouveau riche* still pay lip service to this long and glorious intellectual and cultural tradition which they're all proud of. And the Chinese are much more interested in business than going to nightclubs to show off their wealth and power. I mean, they definitely do show off their wealth, but it's more to prove they've been successful rather than as an end in itself. It's why the Chinese are so successful here. They make millions of dollars, and pay their Khmer protectors a few thousand to run around and play with guns. The Khmers are happy because they can wave their guns around and sleep with nightclub girls, and the Chinese just rake in the money."

A teacher who has lived in Viet Nam points out that, "The Vietnamese—uncultured greedy bastards that they are—at least they still appreciate skill, not just raw power. Like when I would go to the pool, these guys would try to show me up by outswimming me. I happen to be a good swimmer so I always won. Wouldn't matter if the guy was son of the police chief, he'd still respect the fact that I was a better swimmer. Of course, that didn't stop them from going into my locker to steal my wallet. But in Cambodia, they don't respect anything but raw power. If I beat the police chief's son in the pool, he wouldn't care. After all, he could just put a bullet through my brain, and then I wouldn't swim so well, would I."

Dan continues, "And think of how the whole idea of patriotism has been corrupted; when the country's been in civil war for the past twenty-five years, both sides are patriotic and both sides are killing other Khmers. During the Vietnamese occupation, it was possible to be nationalistic and kill invading Vietnamese. But really for most of the past twenty-five years, being a 'good soldier' has meant killing other Khmers. So, no wonder patriotism's a meaningless concept. It's just a pretext for power over other Khmers. It's not too difficult to imagine in fifty years Cambodia won't even exist at all. It'll just be swallowed completely by Thailand and Viet Nam. I've had some students say they see no realistic alternative."

When one of the assembled voices doubts that Cambodia could ever actually disappear, the Bangkok-based journalist responds, "It's not all that hard to imagine a gradual disappearance. For example, the CPP forced their 'compromise' after they lost the election by threatening a secession of seven provinces bordering Viet Nam. It was ludicrous, but it worked because the UN and Sihanouk backed down. They couldn't risk it. But what if they hadn't and the CPP really tried to split— it would've been an autonomous country at war with the rest of Cambodia. It would only have been a few days before Vietnamese troops were inside Cambodia saying they're there at the request of their freedom fighting comrades. And then just a couple of years before the provinces would be absorbed into Viet Nam—certainly in reality, and probably on paper too. The same kind of thing could happen in Western Cambodia. Ieng Sary [the Khmer Rouge's 'Brother Number Two'], demanded—and got—virtual autonomy for splitting from the Khmer Rouge and joining the government. So far, he's been able to maintain independence, because there've been no serious disagreements with Phnom Penh. But if there was some kind of conflict and Phnom Penh sent troops to his region, you can imagine what might happen. He'd ask Thailand for help, and the Thais would do it—they'd do anything to get that area and all the timber and gems. The *baht* is already legal tender up there."

As disheartening as it is to watch a country destroy itself, Cambodian politics also provides some opportunities for laughter. Perhaps the single most tragicomic incident occurs during my December trip to Cambodia. Joe presents us with a copy of the December 14–28 issue of the Phnom Penh Post, showing the thuggish Prime Minister Hun Sen—a man with the mentality and moral stature of a Mafia don—accepting a "Peace Prize." For the past couple weeks, Phnom Penh has been abuzz because an unknown organization awarded Hun Sen this prize for his efforts toward peace. In the US it would carry all the prestige of say, Albert Einstein receiving an honorary membership in the Wichita Falls Junior High School Science Club. But this is Cambodia, and things are different here. Joe is talking animatedly. "I can't believe this. A peace prize for Hun Sen. It's a fucking joke! It has to be. And the Cambodians don't understand that it's *not* the Nobel Peace Prize. Listen to this." Joe begins reading an article from the paper;

> *The honors were to be awarded by the World Peace Corps (WPC), based in Korea and incorporated in the United States. A magnificent honor from an impressive organization, no doubt, although nobody seemed to know much about it. "I've never heard of them," said a spokesman from the US Embassy. "I'm not sure, but I think they might be Moonies," said the head of South Korea's Mission to Cambodia. "We are not Moonies," volunteered a spokesman for the group, contacted in Korea by the Post. "We are independent and we decided to consider Hun Sen for the prize after a recommendation from our man in Phnom Penh."*
>
> *"So who is your man in Phnom Penh?"*

Here Joe imitates a nervous Korean accent for the man's elusive response;

> *"Oh, so sorry. That is a secret—he does not want people to know who he is."*
> *"Why?"*
> *"So sorry."*
> *"OK, then, perhaps you can tell me who exactly is the World Peace Corps?"*
> *"We decide who should get the prize which is sponsored by the Interdenominational Organization. It is free*

41

of religion, race and politics—it will bring peace to the world."

"Free of religion? But a World Peace Corps brochure produced for this event is full of religious references, including that Jesus Christ is the only King of Peace, and that the ultimate goal of the Peace Corps is going back to the bible."

"Ah, so sorry—you fax questions, OK? Good-bye," the spokesman said. Not much luck either in the WPC brochure. Certainly no leads in the printed words of Baron Vaea, Prime Minister of the Tonga Kingdom and Commanding General of World Mongolians.

"Baron Vaea of the World Mongolians?" interrupts an Australian, "this is too much." Joe smiles and says, "Oh yeah, it gets better." He adopts a serious, matter-of-fact tone for this section;

Well, what of the prize itself? The brochure provides the following explanation: "Peace Corps Service Prize, Appreciation Plaque and Certificate. Prize does not pay any sum of funds but provide required assistance to the recipient needs which is kept in strict secrets. Metal [sic] is provided to wear in the event of necessity. The Prize-winner is regarded as family member of Peace Corps and protective efforts provided when necessary. Those who are recommended by the Prize winner may be provided with the required services in the international finance with High Technology." Confused? No matter. In Cambodia, the details are often fuzzy. It's the ceremony which is important. And so, on the day of this auspicious event, Phnom Penh's Chatamouk Theater was sealed off behind a cordon of road blocks and heavily armed soldiers. As Hun Sen's cavalcade wailed closer, a military honor guard—resplendent in shiny helmets, crisp khaki uniforms and natty orange scarves— 'slouched' to attention. The great man alighted from his highly polished limousine. Brandishing automatic weapons, their webbing bulging with spare magazines, his body-

guards whisked Cambodia's man of peace past the kneeling girls into the auditorium.

"Of course, he'd use this peace prize bullshit as a show of force. How could it be any other way?" notes a Canadian teacher with painful irony in her voice. Joe nods his agreement and continues;

*The dissonance seemed lost on the assembled crowd--
complete with the ambassadors of the US, Britain,
Canada, Russia, Viet Nam and other foreign dignitaries
dutifully present—who greeted Hun Sen's arrival with
great applause as he mounted a stage flanked by freshly
picked flowers. He first knelt for a blessing by Buddhist
monks and then seated himself on the stage, with the
crowd continuing the applause. A large Korean gentleman
approached the microphone. The crowd hushed.
"Soksabai," (hello) he said to enthusiastic applause, before assembling a choir who sang what sounded like a
Korean hymn with gravelly gusto. Then the speeches,
most delivered in Korean without translation. "Who are
these guys anyway?" a Foreign Ministry official was overheard asking a Western journalist. An answer, of sorts was
given by one Dr. Robert Leggett, a former US Congress-
men and co-founder of the World Peace Corps Council;
"Honorable judges, doctors and ambassadors, and particularly our new doctor Hun Sen and your lovely wife,
distinguished Buddhist monks, and the people of the great
Republic of Cambodia," he began. A couple of diplomats
exchanged a furtive glance, but did not feel the need to
point out that the Kingdom of Cambodia is a constitutional
monarchy. Leggett began his speech with this disclaimer:
"When the words Peace Corps are applied to the council
. . . they are in no way associated with the American Peace
Corps . . . ." Leggett then listed Hun Sen's many achievements: "[He helped] lay out the Cambodian Constitution,
which amazingly parallels the American Constitution . . .
[it] guarantees the right to strike, to speak, to assemble*

*as we are here today, to publish, and to enjoy religious
worship.*

Joe looks up for a moment. "The right to publish; tell that
to the journalists who were killed or beaten, or the newspapers that've been ransacked. And this next part is rich." He
goes on;

*"The facility for compromise and accommodation of
Minister Sen is well recognized in . . . your Constitution.
The idea of two Prime Ministers to satisfy the two major
factions of the country is much like the Democrat President and the Republican Congress in the US."*

"Yeah, just like if the Democrat President loses the election and calls out the army. Then he has a compromise with
Congress to stay in power despite losing," snorts an American. Joe continues reading;

*The US ambassador remained diplomatically impas-
sive. Others in the audience appeared to have gone to
sleep. Leggett continued ". . . we salute you in Korea . . .
uh. . . . Cambodia, and your Constitution and your economic
and social development and in the area of human rights.
We could use some Sen thinking in America!" Thunder-
ous applause. Those sleeping woke with a start and without much further ado, Hun Sen was awarded his prize and
Ph.D. Then, what seemed to be half the audience moved
forward to present him with bunches of flowers. The entire ceremony was beamed live on television and radio
around Cambodia; the reaction of its audience—anyone's
guess. "Everyone thinks it's a Nobel Prize or something,"
grumbled one government official later. "Yes, yes, yes,"
muttered a by-now exasperated journalist, "but who are
these guys?"*

Joe puts down the paper. "Well, there it is. Typically Cambodian. This evil bastard's been awarded a prize for peace.

By the fucking Commanding General of the World fucking Mongolians, no less. And the Khmers just lap it up like it were serious."

Months later, I speak with a Khmer about Hun Sen's July 1997 power grab. In naive sincerity, the Khmer defends Hun Sen's good intentions, citing the peace prize as his key evidence. It is a sad but typical commentary on Cambodian politics.

Bon Om Teuk (The Water Festival) November 30, 1996

My lessons on the bitterness and brutality of Cambodian history add a definite measure of poignancy to my observations around the city. Bon Om Teuk, for example, is a grand experience in its own right. But it takes on another level of significance when I consider the context. The Water Festival, or more accurately translated, the Racing Boat Festival, is a colorful occasion. Villagers from all over the country pour into Phnom Penh, and the city will be quite crowded. I spent the morning at the guesthouse but now, in the afternoon, the time has come to walk toward the river.

Even at Norodom Boulevard, five kilometers from the riverside, I can feel the crowds. The police have the area roadblocked to prevent the throng of pedestrians from being overwhelmed by motorbikes and cars. As I approach the roadblock, I recall the story passed on by Jimmy, an English teacher, at the guesthouse this morning. He lives in a house between Norodom and the river. When he left this morning, his landlady warned him to bring proof of his address so he could return home with his motorbike. When he got to the roadblock on his way home, a policeman, beer in hand and slurring his words at 11:00 am, demanded $2 to let him through. Jim kept his cool and, by appealing to the sober policemen there, got waved through. I have no such hassles as I pass through the roadblock and continue into the dense crowds on the riverside.

45

The riverbank area is packed with people. Still, I am able to find a place on the riverside promenade to sit and watch the races. Two at a time, long, sleek, and beautifully colored and decorated boats are propelled past me by eager oarsmen, some standing, some sitting, and some kneeling. They, in turn, are driven by a drum-beating coxswain. At the end of each race, the boats are rowed slowly back toward a main collection point. The drums are still beating, but now most of the oarsmen are not rowing. Standing up, they are joyously amusing the crowds with their traditional Khmer celebration dances. Their huge smiles are easily visible from the shore, and it is all very moving. These people have saved all year in order to build their boats and come to Phnom Penh to demonstrate their skills. The sight of them dancing in their craft on the way down the river is one of the most joyous, life-affirming spectacles I have ever seen. As the afternoon wears on, and as boat after boat streams down the river, I break for dinner.

Business as usual at Bhase's. I stuff myself on spicy Tamil food, and then sit back to listen to the sounds of Indian music coming from the TV. The combination of the spices, the music, and the crowds at the riverside has a vaguely hallucinogenic effect. As I head outside—the sun has set during dinner—I glance up at the sign and wonder what that fork and spoon might be saying about me.

Back at the river, the races are over but the crowds have actually intensified. I walk along, inland from the river, and reach a large sound stage sponsored by Fosters Beer. To a large and forgiving audience, amateur singers are crooning their versions of Khmer pop songs. In an increasingly homogeneous world, it is wonderful to see the audience grooving to tunes which draw so heavily on traditional Khmer music. I continue down the road and pass two more stages, barely out of sound's reach of each other; these are co-sponsored by various cigarette and beer companies.

Turning back towards the river, I come to a different sort of stage. Sitting on a patch of dirt by the walkway is a group of six beggars. Four of them are blind and the other two are children. They are all playing traditional Khmer instruments, and some are singing. It sounds improvised because it never stops—flowing continuously in mournful slides up and down the Khmer musical scale. The music is haunting, and as clichéd as that word is, no other description comes close to doing justice to the beautiful sounds I hear. They are softly playing and singing, hoping to earn enough small change to survive another day. I cannot judge their technical ability, or the authenticity with which they are rendering the beauty of traditional Khmer music, but with the mournfully exquisite tunes in my ears and the sight of the huge Cambodian riverfront sky above these six destitute musicians, I know that I will never again be so moved by listening to music. After listening for a long, long time, I leave what I hope will be a significant donation and move on.

Further down the river near the Royal Palace area, is a dazzling light display. A series of barges are moored to the side of the river, each with a 25-foot-high sculpture of light shining brightly into the night. I instantly recognize the first one as a huge map of Cambodia fashioned out of thousands of light bulbs. The Mekong and Cambodia's Great Lake, the Tonle Sap, are illuminated in a blaze of blue. Phnom Penh, Battambang, and other cities are stars shining in white. The outlines of each of the provinces are spidery lines of green. The map is stunningly beautiful, and it can only represent the hope of a brighter future; as this country's past and present remain infinitely darker than the display before me.

The next barge presents the Royal Emblem, all in golden white light. The grandeur of this barge stands in contrast to the ineffectual monarch who was deposed in 1970, led the Khmer Rouge to power, and was then imprisoned by them while they destroyed his country and murdered his subjects. Moving on, I pass another barge which grandly displays a symbol reminiscent of the scales of justice. I cannot read the script, but if this barge is indeed meant to symbolize the bright light of truth and justice, then the irony of it here—in this corrupt, thuggish, Mafia-state—is beyond mention.

47

Off the Rails in Phnom Penh

Two final barges are the only platforms whose bright displays correlate at all with the institutions they represent. A great colorful Hanuman—the monkey-king from the Indian epic, The Ramayana—*is perfected in reds, greens, blues, yellows, golds, and whites. He holds a long sword above his head. This is the symbol of the Royal Cambodian Armed Forces. Moored next to it is a barge with an enormous golden anchor with a long, powerful nine-headed serpent—the naga—entwined around it in blazing white; it represents the Navy. Fueled by foreign aid, illegal weapons sales, smuggling of drugs, timber, and other goods, illegal logging, and child and other prostitution, these institutions—or more accurately, the leaders of these institutions—are shining examples of economic success in Cambodia. Never mind that it is all at the expense of the country they are supposedly defending.*

It is impossible to go further, for I have reached the area where the two Prime Ministers will watch more boat races tomorrow. One of the policemen guarding the area is equipped with an electric stun baton. He plays with his toy, pretending to zap some of his mates around him. Although they are larking around, I can't help drawing an ironic parallel; this game as a typical example of Khmer abuse of power.

Heading back inland through the crush of people, I pass a large blanket spread out on the grass piled with animal hides and bones, snake skins, and other assorted animal leftovers. The 'sponsors' of this particular display are four Montagnards (hilltribe members) from the north, in Phnom Penh for the festival. The blanket looks like a cross between an American Indian fur trading outpost and a medieval witch's laboratory.

I'm still marveling at the cornucopia of animal parts in front of me when the fireworks begin. This is my first opportunity to watch people who have never seen fireworks before enjoy the spectacle. It is amazing to feel their wonder, to hear "oohs" and "aahs"—so tongue-in-cheek in the West—said so sincerely here. I watch the dark, sun-beaten faces of the folks around me as the fireworks burst overhead, and I see those wide Khmer smiles as bright as the barges on the river. All this in spite of, or perhaps because of, 25 years of brutal civil war, repressive dictatorship, and economic stagnation. I am overwhelmed by a sense of humanity here, as if all of us rushing around in modern cities like New York or Bangkok are automatons who have given up some important piece of ourselves to join the modern world. It has always bothered me when rich Westerners romanticize the lives of subsistence farmers—and I realize that for most of the year, these people endure lives of consistent poverty. But watching them watch the fireworks, I can't help but think that they have something which I lack.

The fireworks are over, and I begin heading home. As I walk along Street 178 with the families walking or cycloing home alongside me, I am confronted by the sight of the red fluorescent lights and the girls, sitting in chairs along the doorways, enticing customers. I wonder how it feels for the nine or ten-year-old Khmer boy walking alongside his parents to see these 15 or 18-year-old Vietnamese girls selling their bodies. It's been a long, interesting, and exhausting day, and all my tired brain can come up with as I plod home is, "What a bizarre and intoxicating little country this is."

Lawlessness

"I wasn't worried [about the pistol] yet; it's just another pissed up Khmer impressing the two-dollar whores with what a powerful motherfucker he is."

It is hardly surprising that a government as absurd and incoherent as Cambodia's would have difficulty fulfilling such a necessary function as law and order. Throughout my time in Phnom Penh, I was fascinated by the sensational tales of gunfire and violence, as well as by the attitude of the Majestic regulars toward the anarchy around them. While the lawlessness scares away many tourists and potential investors, for the Majestic crowd it is, perversely, one of the main attractions of Phnom Penh.

It quickly became clear that many of the guys actually get a thrill out of living in this 'Wild West' atmosphere. This feeling of random violence and proximity to death helps turn an otherwise meaningless day conjugating verbs in class into an adventure of urban survival. There is a feeling of bravado from residing in Phnom Penh and living to tell about it. This is especially so since people back home have an exaggerated notion of how dangerous Phnom Penh actually is. Finally, there is simply a visceral excitement of being so close to violence. A trip to the cinema with a group of the Majestic regulars to see *Clear and Present Danger* provides a typical example. One scene takes place in a nightclub in Columbia.

The place is full of gangsters with guns, other sleazy looking characters, and rough looking whores. The director is trying to impress how lawless and dangerous Columbia is. One of the Majestic group turns to us and says, "Oh yeah, I was just thinking about it before, but now it's definite—I'm gonna go to Columbia." Steve, an English teacher from Australia immediately replies, "I'll meet you there, man."

But the presence of so many guns, and the frequency of gunfire, is not necessarily an accurate indication of the level of danger. In fact, much of the gunfire that I encountered or heard about was not violent at all. I witnessed one display of firepower which was actually quite beautiful. I was lucky enough to be in Phnom Penh on April 13, the beginning of Khmer New Year. The year officially begins at 10:48 pm, and at precisely that time, I hear people ringing in the moment with firecrackers and fireworks. Stepping out onto the balcony to view the fireworks, I am in for a surprise; the celebratory cacophony turns out to be something else entirely. People in various parts of the city are firing their guns into the air; single shots, rapid fire, something heavier than the usual AK-47. The sight of the tracer bullets rising up into the night sky is undeniably beautiful. If the shot is at a fair distance, these long streaks of red tracer just float up and then fade out into the sky. If the gun is close, it's like watching a shooting star in reverse. This homespun civil war fireworks display is both terrifying and beautiful. I find out later that one person was killed and six were injured by bullets returning to earth. This is an improvement over last year's toll of five dead and 12 wounded.

Another instance of non-violent gunfire occurs during a severe thunderstorm. We are sitting on the porch listening to the furious downpour when we hear one short, sharp thunderclap. It is followed by four more, and now I know I am listening to gunfire. I ask the other guys if there was a shoot-out. Someone explains that, "No, they're just shooting at the sky to scare the thunder clouds away. It's a Khmer tradition. This 'tradition' exists 'cos they'll take any excuse to fire off their weapons." Another teacher tells me just how common it is; "I was teaching at Monivong [English School] one day when a storm started in the middle of class. Three guys got up and went to the window. They fired off three or four rounds each, and then sat down again. Everyone acted like it was the most normal thing to do."

Clear skies offer as good an opportunity for non-violent gun action as thunderstorms. A long-time teacher relates a lengthy episode about a picnic at Kien Svay he went on with his Khmer girlfriend, Mom. Kien Svay is a resort area on the Mekong about seven kilometers outside the city limits. It is a common place for young, unmarried Khmer couples to go to make love, since tradition and superstition render the family home off-limits for all 'romantic' activity. The teacher begins; "We pass a small cubicle on the right and sit at the table on the patio. We can hear this other couple getting down to it, but we can't see 'cos of the curtains between the two halves of the shack. It's really quite relaxing. It looks out onto the Mekong and there's no traffic noise and a warm breeze.

"Anyway, later—after we've eaten and fucked ourselves stupid—we head for the river. They bring us a full-sized *kromah* and a *sarong* and we walk down the slope out into the sand bars. It's shallow and the current's really slow, barely noticeable. With the *kromah* it's almost like skinny dipping. Mom can't swim at all, but we're having a blast wading in the Mekong with a bellyful of fish.

"Suddenly, these shots ring out and I tense up, ready for a coup or something. Mom just shakes her head and I hear these pissed-up Khmer guys fucking around up on the hill. All I can do is think back to the States; if a bunch of us were hanging out and drinking a few beers, someone would bring out the frisbee or football. Here, they bring out their fucking sidearms. After the first guy started, all his buddies joined in. I wasn't that worried but it wasn't so relaxed after that. Crazy assholes."

While residents become accustomed to guns as toys, this non-violent gunfire can still be unnerving. A teacher tells me of an encounter with a Khmer and his handgun. But first he relates in excruciating detail, and in a completely run-of-the-mill tone, how skillful his Tool Kok prostitute was with her tongue, and how generously his $1 tip complemented the $2 fee. Eventually he gets to his story; "This guy's standing outside the brothel where I'd just shagged these two young things and he's babbling and trying to joke with the girls. He's pissed out of his head and starts waving a pistol around. I wasn't worried yet; it's just another pissed up Khmer impressing the two-dollar whores with what a powerful motherfucker he is. The girls play along and they look a bit scared but I reckon they've been around long enough to know even a fucked-up Khmer is very, very unlikely to start popping people off for no reason. They'll just have a laugh with him—you know what I mean—and maybe shag him until he gets tired enough to put the gun away and piss off home.

"Anyway, my shit-your-pants level went up a notch when he noticed me. I hear this 'oooh' and he points the gun at me and starts slurring something to the girls. I smiled and turned to get out of there but that was a bad move 'cos he fired behind me. I was scared shitless and turned round and saw the arsehole smiling at me and pointing the pistol at the ground.

"I just gave him this smile like, 'Whoa, great joke Dirty Harry. OK, I'm not gonna mess with you.' I don't think he got the message 'cos he fired again and started grinning like an idiot. Then he turned to the girls trying to get them to join in the fun. They're more nervous now so they're laughing along and I give the fucking twat a full on *sompiah* [placing the palms together in front of one's mouth and nose in the traditional Khmer greeting] and say, '*Ban, k'nyom trou tou p'taya.*' [*OK*, I have to go home now]. He rolled up laughing—totally surprised I could speak Khmer—and actually gave me a *sompiah* with the gun still in his hand. I thought 'thank fuck for that,' hoping he'd blow his own fucking head off by mistake. '*Tou p'taya,*' [go home] he goes, and shoots another round in the air. We both laughed like it was some fucking brilliant private joke and I was out of there. What a total fuckwit arsehole!"

With all these examples of gunfire as entertainment, it is encouraging to discover that guns in Phnom Penh can serve a more constructive purpose than simply as macho playthings. One morning, I am woken up by the sound of gunshots close by. Is this the coup that everyone has been expecting? In fact, it turns out to be a house fire, or rather, a shack fire down the block. A resident explains that firing into the air is the accepted way to call for a fire truck. With so many guns and so few phone lines, it is the most effective system. The gunfire works well; the police and fire trucks arrive quickly, and the blaze is under control before the entire block is consumed.

But of course, not all gunfire is so innocuous. The easy access to weapons, and the culture that allows—even encourages—their use, results in far too many examples of death and destruction. But in Cambodia, even gunfire in anger contains a touch of the insane. A classic example is provided by two teachers, Jeff and Avi, who work for the national airline, Royal Air Cambodge. "Yeah," Avi jokes over dinner, "we're gonna start basic weapons training with the first-level classes, and live-fire drills with the level-two classes."

Steve, also at the table, adds that, "I'm going down to be fitted with my official Royal Air Cambodge flak jacket tomorrow." I understand the laughter only when Jeff shows me an article in the paper;

Theng Boon Ma Shoots Off More Than His Mouth to RAC

Theng Boon Ma, a long-time associate and adviser to Hun Sen, who repeatedly denies accusations that he built his multi-million dollar empire on drug smuggling, became very upset when Royal Air Cambodge could not locate his luggage after a recent flight from Bangkok. According to reports, Mr. Boon Ma asked the bodyguard sent to pick him up if the bodyguard had brought extra weapons. The bodyguard dutifully removed an AK-47 from the trunk of the car. Mr. Boon Ma, accompanied by the bodyguard, then returned to the inside of the terminal and walked onto the tarmac, where he fired at the plane which had brought him from Bangkok. One tire valued at $2,000 was destroyed in the shooting. Mr. Boon Ma does not deny the story. "They give such poor service. If they were my employees, I would

*have shot them in the head." Mr. Boon Ma also acknowl-
edged that the only thing that prevented him from doing
more damage to the airplane was that "it was dark and I
couldn't see if there were passengers in the way." Airport
security refused to comment on the fact that the two men
openly brought weapons past customs and immigration
control onto the tarmac. Police officials contacted by this
newspaper acknowledge that Mr. Boon Ma's actions were
illegal, but concede that they have no plans to arrest him.*

More tragic, but no less demented, is a typical story from
an UNTAC veteran about the days when UNTAC was part of
the police force. He tells us about, "This poor, poor general.
You have to feel so bad for him. He was taking a nap in the
afternoon and a neighbor has the nerve to make repairs on
his own house while the general is sleeping next door. The
bastard woke this poor general up in the middle of his nap.
What would you do? Of course, shoot the guy in the head.
Well, that's what this general did. I was on assignment with
the Civilian Police contingent at the time, and we went to in-
vestigate. The guy took off 'cos he figured, 'UNTAC is here,
and I can't just kill people anymore.' We tried to find him, but
everyone was too scared and nobody gave us any help."

Foreigners are not immune to the violence. On my first
day in Cambodia, a resident gives me a sort of a crime rundown. He explains that, "Sure, you see all the soldiers walking around with AK-47s and M-16s, but they almost never
shoot them. In the countryside, they charge 'tolls' at checkpoints and stuff, but you hardly ever see that here [in Phnom
Penh]. One time, someone was shot and killed on the road
around from the guesthouse. Yeah, it was disturbing to see
the body lying there, but it wasn't a random killing, and nobody else was hurt. Oh yeah, and at the guesthouse around
the corner, a German guy and two Khmers were killed by a
grenade. I never got the full story, but it was something about
the German guy being involved with someone else's wife.
Anyway, there's only been a couple of times where I've ever
felt in danger. Probably the worst was a few months ago.

Some guy stole a motorbike and was driving off down Monivong. The police started firing at him while I was just in front of them. It was loud, but I don't think they hit anyone. I wasn't hurt anyway. And take the recent robberies. Put it this way; everyone I know had a gun pointed at them, but nobody I know got hurt. Anyway, that three month stretch of muggings is over. Apparently, it was some Chinese-Khmer who was renting out guns to all these policemen's sons. They threw him in jail and got all the guns back. It was hairy for those couple of months but now there're very few robberies at all. So don't worry."

An English teacher from New York offers more reassurance; "I feel safer here than back home. I mean, there're muggings in both places, but there's a big difference. Shit, back home, you can hand over your money, and still get shot. Maybe just 'cos the guy's on crack, or he has to earn points with his gang by taking someone out, who the fuck knows. Here, you get held up, but as long as you hand over the cash, no-one's gonna get hurt."

But there are sometimes robberies that end in tragedy. Tourists, as opposed to residents, are especially prone to violence because they are more likely to carry a lot of money with them, and then resist when confronted by armed robbers. In a typical episode, a tourist refused to hand over his backpack to robbers. His friend, coming over to assist, ended up getting shot and killed. The guys at the Majestic—speaking contemptuously about the tourist—sound like hardened war veterans denigrating the raw new recruits. The main reaction, besides scorn, is bad taste. One teacher jokingly paraphrased the hapless tourist who got his friend killed; "My camera isn't worth my life, but it sure is worth my buddy's life."

Other tragedies can—and do—hit residents. The Majestic is in a flurry the morning after one robbery. The victim explains; "Malai [his Khmer girlfriend] and I were on our way back from Champagne when we got held up by these three assholes. It all went fine until the cops showed up and opened fire, and these three started firing back. We hit the ground.

After the cops had killed them, I saw Malai was bleeding. She got hit in the stomach by a ricochet. She's still in the hospital."

Another morning, I listen to the residents trade theories about the violent death of a volunteer English teacher in a village outside of Phnom Penh. Reiner gets out a Phnom Penh Post and reads parts of the article;

> *Richard Fernando, 26, of the Philippines was killed in Kandal province half an hour's drive from Phnom Penh, when he tried to stop a student from throwing a grenade. He took the full brunt of the blast . . . He was trying to restrain an unruly student who had threatened to throw the grenade at other students. Sister Denise Coghlan, the director of the organization which runs the school for the disabled where Fernando was killed, said that, "Richie died holding the man in his arms as they fell to the floor. The man got up unharmed, Richie died instantly. His brave action probably saved the lives of many. The student got on his bicycle and surrendered to the police immediately. He is absolutely remorseful for what happened."*

Cries of "stupid fucker" resound as Reiner continues;

> *She cautioned people not to be quick to condemn the behavior of the disabled Cambodian, saying it was important to understand his circumstances. "A veteran of Cambodia's wars, and an orphan of Pol Pot's regime, on the morning of Fernando's death, he had been reprimanded for playing cards with a new student."*

Reiner stops reading and two emotions dominate the conversation. The teachers are relieved that there is not, suddenly, some organized campaign against their profession—but rather, the volunteer died while consciously intervening in a dangerous situation. They are also thrilled yet again at this 'Wild West' atmosphere they live in. Some of the longer-term residents describe other incidents of gunfire, violence and death. Only the newspaper article expresses any regret over the young Filipino volunteer's violent end.

But even when there are no explosions or gunfire, it does not guarantee that everything is peaceful; the threat of violence is at least as common as its application. For many of my perspectives on Khmer society, I turn to Reiner and Dara. Dara is a Khmer who works for Reiner as a combination Khmer teacher and 'gopher.' This very amiable and gentle man also happens to work for the Ministry of Defense. As with many other government employees, Dara shows up at the office one or two hours a day in order to earn his $16 per month salary and, more importantly, maintain his place within patronage networks. The remainder of his time is devoted to earning a living. One morning, I come down to the restaurant to find Dara talking animatedly to Reiner, who gives me the general drift. The water utility is carrying out pipe repairs in the area of Dara's house. Such maintenance work is usually financed by cutting the water supply of the neighborhood until each house has 'contributed' to the repair costs. Dara was not surprised when they arrived for the money, but he was taken aback by the size of their 'request.' Because Dara's extended family has a large house, the water 'mafia' demanded an outrageous $300, which was simply too extortionate. The usual scenario is that Dara can either pay up or live without water, but on this occasion he gets four privates from his regiment to 'stand guard' around one of the water company's vehicles. If Dara does not get his water, then the water company does not get their equipment back.

Reiner walks Dara out of the restaurant and then comes back to finish the story. "He was in a hurry to get back to his house. The soldiers are young and 'excitable'—I guess that's the best translation. He said he wants to get back before there're any tense arguments and they end up shooting someone."

The next day, Reiner relates the results; "It actually ended very peacefully. The water guys compromised, and they settled on a hundred dollars, which was acceptable to everyone.

No shooting, no injuries, and, according to Dara, not really much arguing either. See, Khmers can be reasonable."

Another episode settled with the threat—but not the use of violence, happened just after New Year. Steve tells me how, "I saw people in front of the house all looking down toward Hong Kong Center [a modern four-story building which is Phnom Penh's only multi-purpose entertainment-shopping-office complex]. I got dressed and went down to take a look. I see eight of the heavy-duty police bikes collecting around the far end of the Center—you know, the entrance to The Base [nightclub] and the Carriana [casino]. Each bike brought two cops with two automatic rifles, mostly AKs. These cops aren't celebrating—they set up a perimeter around the area keeping an eye outwards, probably in case whoever they're here for calls for his own back-up.

"A businessman and two partners come out with the head cops. The guy looks Chinese—or Chinese-Cambodian—and I reckon the two cops are in charge. There's all sorts of conferring going on—the guy talking with the cops, and his cronies on their hand phones, and the cops are busy with their walkie-talkies. Except for the other cops with guns on the perimeter, it all looks pretty friendly. If anyone's tense or scared, they aren't showing it. Eventually the cops relax the perimeter and roar off on their bikes and the guys go back to business inside the Center.

"Too bad my Khmer's nowhere near good enough to ask anyone what was going on. I guess they were there collecting a debt, a bribe, or some other back-hander. Whatever it was, it ended quietly."

That the police were out probably settling a private commercial argument raises an interesting question about the role of the police force. They cannot be accused of idleness. Eric, another teacher from Switzerland, tells me of often seeing the police cruise by the brothels collecting cash at each one, although he has never been able to see how much. Prostitution is categorically illegal in Cambodia, but for the police the difference between enforcement and extortion is not very clear. Often, they collect more than protection money.

Eric tells me of one night in a brothel, saying, "We were hang-ing out in the brothel" with the same expression I use to say, "We were hanging out at the bar." After describing his dis-appointment with the young girl whose services he pur-chased, he tells me about sitting with Steve, and Steve's girlfriend Lan, who works in the brothel. "Suddenly, all the girls by the door run inside. Lan and my girl stand up, ready to take off and the mamasan runs to the doors to close them. I get up to see, and my girl pulls me back. I don't hear any gunshots, so I go to have a look. I'm crouching next to the mamasan and look out the door. This police truck's stopped at a brothel five or six houses down the street."

The type of truck Eric is talking about is a common sight in Cambodia. It is a pickup with two benches placed back to back in the flatbed area. The truck can carry a lot of men all at once; the police or soldiers can sit on these benches relatively com-fortably, and they can also be ready for action very quickly. Indeed, the police in this truck have deployed very rapidly into the unfortunate whorehouse.

Eric continues; "Two cops with their AKs ready stand ei-ther side of the brothel entrance. I've no idea how these two got picked for guard duty. I wonder if there's a rotation. Any-way, now that they've chosen their brothel, things in Lan's place calm down. Yeah, so they go in and fuck the girls for an hour or so, get drunk, and then leave without paying a penny. Steve told me it happens in Lan's place every couple of months."

I hear another interesting story from Rick, a teacher, about this nexus between the police and prostitution. "I saw two girls standing in the entrance to the guesthouse. They were real sexy—nice and young, maybe fourteen or fifteen—and they were scared shitless of something. Joe was upstairs so I got him down to translate.

"At first, he thought they wanted us to call the police. Then we figured out it was the cops they were afraid of. Like, they were really scared. It turns out that if they're walking around at night without a regular family to vouch for them, they can be picked up and sold [or rather re-sold] to a new brothel.

You know what that means, they have new debts and lose the credit with the place they're in now. If they can get themselves onto a *moto*, they'll be fine. Usually they'd just risk it and walk to the main street but they saw a bunch of cops on the corner, and they wouldn't go. It was kind of fun acting like older brother. Could just as easily have been shagging them in a brothel. So, I went to get *moto*s to come right to the front of the guesthouse while Joe promised them they'd be back safe(?!) in their brothel in no time."

But the police do more than just extort, rape, and sell young girls. Steve tells me of a teacher at The American-Cambodian Center who was upset at the way a certain well-connected school administrator was misusing donations to her school from the US. As his distaste grew, he let it be known that his next step would be to discuss the matter with Cambodian journalists. That evening, he was visited by four armed policemen and taken down to the jail, where he spent the night. The next day, the very same school administrator came to the jail to inform him that his visa had suddenly expired and he was now to leave the country. Before his flight, he told Steve how the police were actually quite pleasant, except when the school administrator was around, at which times they put on a show of vicious intimidation.

With the police so busy with personal matters, it is up to citizens themselves to handle their own protection. Through Dara and Reiner, I learn about the private security that the rich and powerful use to defend themselves in the absence of any organized law and order. The Toyota Landcruiser is the vehicle of choice for the wealthy and powerful. One very common option is tinted windows—so no one can see which particular general or businessman is cruising down the street. Another option, though less common than tinted windows, is a pair of gun-toting bodyguards driving alongside the rear passenger side window on a powerful motorbike.

I listen as Dara gives a rundown of what it costs for a full complement: two guys inside the car, and two guys each on two motorcycles on either side. Their salaries are $400 each per month, meaning $2,400 a month for the manpower. But to equip them is a huge investment. Dara gives us a general idea, and Reiner lays it out;

Motorcycles	2	@	$3,000	= $6,000
Cell Phones	6	@	$800	= $4,800
Sidearms	6	@	$200	= $1,200
Grenades	12	@	$40	= $480
ICOMs (walkie-talkies)	3	@	$150	= $450
AK-47s	4	@	$100	= $400
Bullets—AK-47	360	@	.2	= $72
Sidearm	120	@	.75	= $80
Accessories (cuffs, holsters, etc.)				= $300

So, for an initial outlay of almost $15,000, plus $2,400 a month, you can buy yourself a full complement of bad-ass bodyguards. Dara provides more information through Reiner; "They love to fight, they love to work out and practice, but they have to remain cool. There's nothing worse than a body-guard starting a fight without orders from his boss. They ride around hoping for someone to fire so they have the perfect excuse to fight back. The pay's great, but it's a tough life as well. There are no hours—anytime the boss needs them, they're on duty. And it's dangerous, too. They're skilled, but their potential opponents are also skilled, maybe more so. A lot of them have nightclub girls for wives. They have the money to go to the clubs, and parents of straight girls won't let them marry a bodyguard. They're too afraid of their daughters being left without a husband. You know, a lot of times, they don't even know who they're working for. The big boss will sit in the car, and give orders through the phones or ICOMs or through the bodyguards inside the car. But he won't show his face to the guys on the outside."

Dara and Reiner have now touched on something that has puzzled me for a while. With private armies running around, armed to the teeth and looking for action, how can there be a moment of peace in the city? What prevents them from simply looting everything and raping or beating everyone in sight? Dara is puzzled by my question but Reiner manages to clarify the situation; "They are employees, not bandits. If someone owes the boss money they'll go into his house and take his stuff. If someone pisses the boss off, they'll beat him up or kill him. But to go out on their own and just steal a TV for the money, no way. Even the guys that kill for a living, it's not just a question of money. If someone hires this guy to kill you, there's no way you can buy your way out of it with the killer, no matter how much you offer. He's accepted his money to do the job, and he'll do it. You may be able to buy your way out with the guy who assigned the killer, or you can hire a killer to get to the other guy first, but you can't bribe out the guy assigned to you.

"These bodyguards just don't do random stealing or kill-ing. First of all they and the police all know each other. As long as there's a reason for what's happening, no-one's go-ing to be arrested. But the police know that if people start going on random stealing sprees, the whole society will break down. They won't let that happen because it means very quickly there'll be nothing left to steal. Don't worry. As long as you stay out of their way, and out of the way of the boss, none of these guys will hassle you. In fact, if they see you being robbed by real criminals, it's very likely they'll jump at the excuse to get into action and execute the criminals them-selves."

This explanation raises an important point in understand-ing Phnom Penh's mayhem—the distinction between random violence and revenge. A young Canadian who runs a bar in Phnom Penh offers an example of this contrast. "These mini-militias, or whatever you want to call them, don't really steal out of greed. But they're not saints, that's for sure. I had a TV and VCR ever since I opened up three years ago. All that time, no problems. Then last April, I fired this waitress. I mean, she was lazy. Even the other Khmers thought she was use-less, and that's saying something. Anyway, two days after I fired her, this car pulls up, and four guys jump out. They all had their AKs, and one even had a grenade belt. One guy points his gun at me, another aims at everyone else in the bar. The other two went straight for the TV cabinet. We know she told them where it was 'cos they knew exactly where to look.

"The police I deal with explained it like this; the protection money I pay them is for protection against '*to-a-ma-da*' [ordinary] crime. But this was '*pi-say*' [special]. Everyone here knows someone with access to weapons. If you piss someone off enough, they *will* get back at you."

For ordinary Khmers, who cannot afford private armies, self-enforcement seems to be the common rule. One day, Dara comes into the Majestic, flustered. He apologizes to Reiner for coming late and then goes into a long explanation. Reiner translates; "Two guys tried to steal a motorbike from his neighbor. The neighbor noticed and yelled out, so everyone in the neighborhood came running. One guy got away, but the mob caught the other one and beat him to death."

While most Khmers simply do the best they can to survive in this world of violence, many foreigners get drawn into it. Eric is a perfect example. He relished being drafted into the Swiss Army, and with equal verve and eloquence, he declares his contempt for "homosexual perverts," and his joy at purchasing sex from 14-year-old girls. The climate of political violence thrills Eric. Over dinner one evening, I listen to Rick and Eric discuss Cambodian politics—or more specifically, how one of its main players can be eliminated. The Swiss monotone declares that, "Hun Sen, that worthless piece of communist shit, doesn't even deserve a proper assassination. He should be shot down in the jungle and wounded and left to die. But that won't happen, so we need to have a regular assassination."

"But how?" asks Rick earnestly.

Eric responds, "If you watch his bodyguards, they like looking very tough with all those machine guns and grenades, but notice their eyes. They just glare a few meters in front of them, never even a glance into the distance. They just don't expect a long-distance attack. When I was at the *Ecole des Recruits* [the Swiss Army basic training center], I volunteered for extra training with sniper rifles. I trained with a Schmidt-Rubens K-31. That could put a bullet through his stupid communist brain. These AKs and M-16s are accurate enough for assassination only to about fifty meters. On a windless day, a sniper rifle is deadly up to six hundred meters. Hun Sen's fucking idiot guards wouldn't have a chance against that. If FUNCINPEC can give me one Schmidt-Rubens and a hundred thousand dollars, I'll guarantee that within one month, Hun Sen goes down."

"I wonder who you talk to about something like that?" Rick asks.

Another discussion shows how serious Eric can be about assassinations. One day at The Majestic, Eric and his housemates are engaged in a loud and heated discussion about their landlady. Eric is furious, and the others are trying to calm him down; "No Eric, it's just a misunderstanding. She didn't say we couldn't bring girls home, she just wants us to be careful."

"I don't care. She's an old cunt. She's always in our business. What does she care if some taxi-girls steal our stuff. It's not her problem. I want her dead."

"Come on, first of all, if something gets stolen and we blame her, then it *is* her problem. Second of all, just tell her we'll be careful, and that's the end of it."

"No. I hated her from the beginning, and I want her dead. It's simple. All we need is two hundred dollars between us. I know someone who can arrange it. Just give him a photograph and the two hundred. Within a week, she's dead."

"Listen Eric, if she dies, we might have to move. Let's just let it be, OK?"

Eric is silent and heads off for home. No one can tell if he has calmed down or if he is planning to finance the assassination himself. "Two hundred dollars?" I ask the guys. Avi responds, "Yeah, that's what I've heard. Although I think it's not that simple. If it's a foreigner, it'd probably be more, and if the target is 'protected' by someone more powerful, there'd have to be more because there's more risk of the police getting involved. Also, it's not all that easy to arrange. After all, you have to pay up front. So if the guy you hire decides not to follow through, what are you going to do? Sue him? I heard about one foreigner who paid three hundred bucks to have his girlfriend's husband killed. He was some ex-soldier asshole who used to keep beating her up. The hit man just took the money and didn't do anything. In fact, it looks like he went and told the husband. So, this guy's out three hundred dollars and scared shitless that the husband's going to come after him. If you're really part of a patronage network, which few foreigners are, then I suppose you could find someone reliable to do a hit."

A bit unsettled I ask, "So at any moment, someone could walk in here and kill me just because someone else paid him two hundred bucks?"

"Have you pissed anyone off lately?"

"Not that I know of."

"Well, you should be fine then. Nobody's going to spend two hundred dollars or whatever to kill you just for the fun of it. There has to be a good reason."

Avi notices from my expression that I am not particularly reassured about this; "It's Phnom Penh," he says with a shrug.

The Firing Range
December 8, 1996

As might be expected from men thrilled with violence, talk is cheap—only action really counts. One of the more dramatic ways to participate in Phnom Penh's Disneyland of violence is at the shooting range near the airport. Unlike the drugs or the brothels, this activity is actually fairly expensive. I accept Eric's invitation to go with a group on one of their infrequent trips to the range. I jump on one of the motorbikes and we head off. Just before the main 'highway' out to the airport is another main east-west road called Kampuchea Krom Street. Eric informs me that, "It was called Cambodia-Viet Nam Street during the Hun Sen regime. You know, to 'commemorate the eternal solidarity and friendship between the fraternal social- ist peoples of Cambodia and Viet Nam'—whose troops hap- pened to have been occupying the country. After the

Vietnamese left and they had the elections, it got a new name—Kampuchea Krom. That means 'Lower Cambodia.' It's what the Khmers call the area the Vietnamese stole from them a couple of hundred years ago."

As we drive on, I recognize the road to the airport from my visa run. The landscape becomes rural surprisingly quickly; mostly open fields and shacks here, but we do see some warehouses and factories that represent the hopes for economic progress.

We soon arrive at the shooting range, which is part of a large, ramshackle army base. We head toward a small building which contains an amazing array of guns and ammunition. This structure opens out onto a large field which is the actual firing area. I watch, amazed, as Eric strokes and inspects the guns. One of the guys in the group jokes that he is more careful selecting a rifle than he is in choosing his brothel whores. "Because renting the rifle is so much more expensive," he retorts. The fee is only $10 an hour for the rental of the gun, but the real financial burden is the ammo—at 25 cents per bullet. Eric assures me that when you see the tracers streak toward the target, it is worth every penny.

We head out to the range and begin firing. The action is leisurely, as the Khmer staff have to pull the paper targets back and forth by hand. But slow is fine, because if the process were any faster, a day at the range would either be terribly short or terribly expensive. The guys are having a ball out here on a sunny day with the smell of the gun oil mixing with the acrid aftertaste of exploded gunpowder. We shoot a few targets on single-fire, and then switch to automatic for the real fun. Eric is in his element, and the action-movie jokes are coming thick and fast. We are joined at the range by a couple of Frenchmen who look to be regulars. They are familiar with the staff and shoot quite well.

The soldiers bring out B-40 rocket launchers and some B-40 grenades, and we take a break to watch as the Frenchmen prepare to shoot the rockets. The target is basically a five-foot-high stake planted into the ground. The objective is not so much to hit the pole as to shred it with the exploding grenade. *The first two shots manage to knock it around, but the third one eviscerates the thing completely. The Khmer staff congratulate the guy who fired the shot, while their associates set up another target.*

There is no doubt now that Eric will have to get into this, and two others in the group, including myself, are also getting itchy trigger fingers. The $35 per shot price tag is hardly an obstacle after the destruction we just witnessed. We shoot off our remaining AK-47 rounds, and then the B-40 contingent steps forward to receive their launchers. Eric can barely sit still for the instructions, and I can hear him almost panting. His shot knocks the stake down, but fails to destroy it; impressive for us, but disappointing for him. Two others fire, and their shots don't even register on the target. After I fire, I can't help but feel an immense rush of power and satisfaction at the knowledge that the huge explosion less than 100 meters away was triggered by my fingers. I have an urge to fire again; to show the world what a mean motherfucker I am, and how anything that stands in my way is going to be blasted out of existence. Khmer men are starting to make more sense to me now.

It was an exhilarating but expensive day at the range, and we collect all our stuff for the ride back to town. Eric is in a state of nirvana-like silence. He manages to explain that, "Shooting rifles isn't such a big deal. Any Swiss who's been through the draft has one at home. I shot plenty at the Ecole. But I've never fired a rocket." He grins all the way back to the Majestic.

Camouflage, Handcuffs, and Schoolgirl Uniforms
April 12, 1997

Eric and Steve are hurriedly slurping down the runny eggs which are known at the Majestic as omelets. Both of them are eager to put their projects in motion. As they explain their respective plans, Steve graciously invites me to come along. I cannot afford to miss another perfect example of how Cam-

bodia's unique circumstances can unhinge its foreign residents.

Eric has long had a fantasy of dressing up in Cambodian army and police uniforms. Steve's fantasy is a bit different, but equally unusual for someone not used to Phnom Penh. In the time since my last trip to Cambodia, Lan, Steve's 16-year-old girlfriend from the brothel, has moved in with him. He has a special fantasy in mind for her. In any other country, this might remain within the realm of wishful thinking. But the defining feature of Cambodia is the incredibly short distance between conceiving a fantasy and making it a reality. Any legal, social, or moral obstacles that might have deterred them in Switzerland and Australia are completely irrelevant here.

Immediately after paying the bill, Eric and Steve get up to leave. Steve revs up his bike, and Eric climbs onto the back of the Honda I have rented for the weekend, and soon our little convoy is heading to the market. Eric is excitedly telling me about his planned purchases; at least two army uniforms, a police uniform, a pair of handcuffs, plus whatever else strikes his fancy. He is unsure what kind of firearms we can get, but is interested to find out. Then he tells me a story from his stay in 1995. "There was this stupid English asshole who was staying at the guesthouse. In class, they were talking about guns and one of his students told him after the lesson he had a gun for sale. This guy went to his student's house with a hundred and fifty dollars and got himself a used and illegal AK-47. OK, you're in Cambodia, you want to buy a gun, that's perfectly reasonable. But this fucking idiot is so happy that he walks back to the guesthouse firing his new toy every few minutes. What a fucking asshole. Anyway, the police were waiting for him by the time he got to the Majestic. They all came out, guns drawn, grabbed the AK, shoved him to the ground, handcuffed him, and gave him a couple of kicks just for being such a fucking idiot. They confiscated the gun. I think they took him to the police station and told him he could either pay a 'fine' of four hundred US and leave the country, or do some time in T3 [the big prison in Phnom Penh]. I guess he had enough money to leave, because I didn't see him after that. What I really hope is that they shot him for being such a stupid cunt."

Fifteen minutes later we arrive at the market located in the northwest outskirts of the city. We go into what looks like a regular market, with the usual collection of food and clothing stalls. Eric, who looks as if he is being drawn by some powerful, primitive urge, leads us to the section we want. Stall after stall offers every kind of police and military accessory imaginable—including uniforms and insignia, all for sale to the general public.

Eric goes first. Too excited to haggle, he chooses and tries on a solid olive-green uniform. Finally, he picks out his insignia and hands it to the stall owner. A few minutes sewing and $11 later, Eric is a corporal in the Royal Cambodian Armed Forces (RCAF).

Steve, meanwhile, has been looking at dress uniforms, and chooses one in dark green. He finds a pair of sunglasses that fit and, with his new uniform on, struts around looking like some Australian Patton ready to kick some ass.

Eric realizes that his uniform is not really complete. He still needs a cap, and it must have the RCAF insignia on it as well. He buys one, and Steve follows suit. "For Lan," he explains with a lewd smile. Eric picks out a second uniform—this one is fully camouflaged fatigues—and he also promotes himself to sergeant. Then for the police uniforms with their own lion insignia.

Now we are ready for the hardware. Eric stops at a stall and starts examining, actually fondling, a pair of handcuffs. Seven dollars later, he places them in their handy, belt-attached carrying pouch, and puts them in his goody bag. Another stall, and an accessory belt soon follows the handcuffs into the bag. Here, the proprietor offers us some deals on merchandise not on display. An AK-47 can be ours at his opening bid of $100. A grenade—US-made, he assures us—is a steal at $20. We can walk home with a Chinese-made land mine for $15. And a handgun is ours for $300. We ponder these tempting bargains, but none of us is ready to make that kind of purchase—at least not yet. I recall the story of a woman who bought a land mine to plant in her yard as protection against thieves. The device exploded on the way home, killing the moto driver who was unfortunate enough to pick up this bad fare.

Eric is satisfied for now, so we move on to Steve's mission. He pulls out a piece of paper with Lan's measurements on it, and heads for the 'civilian' clothing section. He picks out the white blouse and pleated blue skirt that thousands of Cambodian schoolgirls wear every day to school. He cheerfully hands over the $5 and takes possession of the schoolgirl uniform. Eric and Steve are eager to get home with their goodies, and I accept their invitation to come by and see the results. The two of them rush home on Steve's bike and arrive before me.

By the time I come up the stairs to their house, Steve, Eric, and Lan have all changed into their respective uniforms. Eric is in his camouflage fatigues and is chasing Lan around, who looks mighty cute in the schoolgirl outfit. Lan and Eric are laughing loudly, and Eric is declaring that he will handcuff her so Steve can rape her. Steve is swaggering around in his dark green dress uniform and sunglasses, ordering Lan to stand still so Eric can cuff her. Lan is giving Eric a run for his money. At 16, she is energetic, and the years in the rice fields have provided her with a vigorous (and vivacious) vitality. Eric is soon exhausted. Lan and Steve go into Steve's room to make love, and Eric goes into his room, I presume, to masturbate. I chat with Jeff, their third housemate, and the two of us head to the Majestic.

Bloody Sunday
March 30, 1997

The adventurous thrills and jokes about lawlessness and violence all ring hollow after the morning of March 30. It was right at the beginning of my April visit. Steve was out of town, so the guys in his house invited me to stay with them.

Whatever they are, they are loud. Four explosions wake me up, and they sound very close. Even in Phnom Penh it is strange to hear gunfire early on a Sunday morning, and I roll out of bed to see if anything interesting is going on outside. From the porch, I can see people running towards, and away from, the National Assembly building, just 150 meters from the house. I can hear shrieks and screams and cries for help. I hurry back into Steve's room to get dressed, splash some water on my face, and head outside.

Leaving the house, I immediately see two cars stopped in the middle of the road, and a motorcycle lying on the pavement. Was it a traffic accident? I quickly dismiss that thought once I notice perhaps two hundred people running about. As I move closer, I see the blood. Blood on the shirts and pants and faces of countless people.

Soon, I am close enough to witness each individual tragedy. A woman—unconscious or worse—is placed onto a moto by a man. One arm is so bloody that I'm not sure how much of it is left. In order to secure her for the ride, the man flops both her arms—one intact, one torn—around the shoulders of the driver. The driver grabs the uninjured arm with one hand, and speeds off.

On the sidewalk, I see a man face down in a pool of blood. He tries to curl himself up into a ball, but it is almost impossible for him to move. His head is cradled by another man who alternately speaks softly to the man dying on the ground next to him, and pleads for help.

Someone picks up the downed motorbike. It reveals a woman so obviously dead that no one bothers with her while there are still living wounded to be taken care of. Her head lies at an incredibly unnatural angle to her body. Although there is too much blood to see for certain, it looks like her head has been almost completely severed. She lies there but won't be moved until the living have been dealt with.

Half in shock, I shuffle on into the carnage. A man limps toward a cyclo and collapses into it. He is too weak to ask someone to take him. A woman holds the hand of a man ly-

ing on the ground. He bleeds from a seemingly infinite number of wounds. She weeps as he dies.

It is about 20 minutes after the explosions now, and the police that were on hand are only just beginning to take action. They carelessly heave the wounded into the backs of trucks. I see the remains of a woman's mangled legs hanging out the back of one as it drives off. Another policeman takes down a loudspeaker from a tree. A meter away from the tree, a child is staring upward in shock, and bleeding from where his foot used to be. The foot itself lies nearby.

Somehow out of the chaos, all the wounded are evacuated, and then all the dead. Now only the blood and the onlookers remain. The blood and also the placards. Most are in Khmer, but some are in English. "Cambodian People Call for an Independent Judiciary" says one. The "le" in "People" is smudged with blood.

The shops along the street have all shuttered their doors by now. I plod my way back to the house. I wash my hands and my face, then undress and take a shower. Without knowing why, I get back into Steve's unfamiliar bed. I cry.

A few hours later, we exchange information at the Majestic. The Khmer Nation Party, led by prominent dissident Sam Rainsy, organized a demonstration against the CPP-dominated judiciary. Assailants threw four grenades into the crowd of demonstrators. Twenty-five people are dead, and over 100 injured. The men who threw the grenades were seen to run across the park toward the wat opposite Steve's house. Soldiers—identified as part of Hun Sen's personal bodyguard—who were in the park before the demonstrators arrived, let the grenade throwers pass through, but knocked pursuers to the ground. Behind the wat is a CPP residential compound. Also notable was the fact that—as opposed to earlier demonstrations—the police presence was very light, and stood far back from the demonstrators. It was as if they were expecting the attack. While all this clearly implicates Hun Sen as responsible for the carnage, he has publicly called for the arrest of Sam Rainsy, the organizer of the rally for "failing to protect the demonstrators." He states that, "I've asked the Interior Minister to consider whether we should drag the demonstration's mastermind by the neck into court." From the porch of their house, Eric saw an armored personnel carrier wheel its way out of the compound into which the grenade throwers allegedly fled. The cold-bloodedness of the killing is matched by the callousness of the politicking—and for the umpteenth time, it is clear that for Cambodian democracy to live, Hun Sen must die.

The shock of the morning wears off, and the day gives way to depression and gloom. It is yet one more brutal tragedy that Khmers have inflicted against fellow Khmers.

Sex

"She still hasn't forgiven me from the last time in the brothel. I kind of forced her to let me shag her up the ass. It must've hurt, but I gave her a nice tip."

Such things as the beauty of the culture, the rips in the social fabric, or the Machiavellian intrigues of Cambodian politics may be of interest to passing journalists, but there was another aspect of the country's deranged environment that held the tightest grip on most of the regulars at the Majestic. If the proportion of conversations devoted to each topic is an accurate way of ranking them in importance, then cheap sex is by far the most crucial factor in understanding most residents' fascination for Cambodia.

Prostitution is certainly not unique to Cambodia. However, the Cambodian manifestation is mind-boggling in both the overwhelming scale and openness with which it is practiced, and the shockingly low prices at which it is available. Wherever you are in Phnom Penh you are never more than a few minutes away from a place to purchase sex. Unlike other parts of the world where prostitution is hidden behind a veil of massage parlors or nightclubs, Phnom Penh brothels are as obvious as they are numerous—with their pink florescent lights shining out, and the young girls congregating by the door beckoning to passers-by.

Khmer social attitudes are also quite forgiving. The overwhelming majority of Khmer males lose their virginity in a brothel. At a housewarming party given by a Khmer journal-ist, the male guests (all Khmer excepting myself) openly joke—in front of the women—about "Entering Viet Nam. No passport, no visa, just five dollars." While scoffing at other aspects of Khmer culture and society, many foreigners em-brace this facet wholeheartedly. It was a rare conversation at the Majestic that did not include at least some reference to "shagging."

What was most striking about these conversations was the complete lack of discretion or inhibition. Prostitution, which is usually considered morally wrong, exploitative, or at least shameful to partake of in the West, is more or less celebrated at the Majestic. Even in Bangkok, notori-ous for its sleazy bar scene, the raunchy conversations were, for the most part, conducted with a modicum of self-consciousness. And compared to my university in the US, where referring to a 19-year-old female as a *girl* (instead of the politically correct term *woman*) was considered seri-ous sexual harassment—and calling an attractive woman a "babe" would be grounds for castration, the Majestic was a different planet altogether. In just one of thousands of examples of the unparalleled brazenness of the Majestic conversations, I overhear this self-congratulatory conver-sation between a relative newcomer and a brothel veteran. The newcomer begins;

> "It's the firmness that gets you. These young girls with unbelievably flat stomachs, and tits without a hint of sag. That's what's most amazing. It's the firmness."
> "Hey, I think you've found the new slogan for the Cambodian tourism promotion board. Cambodia: It's the Firmness that Gets You. I can see the poster now. A line of girls with miniskirts and halter-tops."
> "Yeah, and for the TV ads, we can have the same girls with these fat, balding French and German sex tour-ists and drooling Chinese businessmen fondling them and they're saying, 'Cambodia: It's the Firmness that Gets You!'"

"And some Australian with a beer gut that's older than the girl. His flab alone weighs more than she does, and he's sticking it into this tight sixteen-year-old."

"I tell ya, these titties that stand up and salute when they take off their bras, smooth curves from head to toe. And when they roll over to take it from behind, not a trace of flab on the thighs and ass cheeks. Yup, it's the firmness that gets you."

Another typical conversation shows how prostitution is not just acknowledged, but openly celebrated over meals and beers at the Majestic;

"It's fucking great. I mean, in the US, I might be running some stupid errand at some strip mall [shopping arcade] and then suddenly think, 'Hmm, I could go for a burger right now.' If there's a burger place in the same mall, OK, I'll stop and get a burger. But if not, I'm not gonna drive around looking for a McDonald's or whatever, I'll just go home. Here it's the same kind of deal, but for sex. Like, OK, it's three o'clock and I have an hour before some boring fucking class. 'Let's see, if I go right now, I'll definitely have time for a fuck.' Or like all the teachers at Monivong [an English school located very close to the 154th Street brothels], 'Hey, I'm here already, I might as well go get a blowjob.'"

"Yeah, you're right. You finish shopping at Central Market, you figure, 'What the hell, stop in for a quick shag [in a brothel] on Sixty-three.'"

"Right, or you can just wait until tomorrow when you've got a long lunch break between classes. Then you don't have to rush the shag so much."

"That's right."

"And you don't have to worry about a schedule. In Phnom Penh, it's any fucking time you want."

"Convenience. Like whorehouse Seven-Elevens."

"Yeah. 'We're open for pussy twenty-four hours a day.' It don't get any better than this."

For many outsiders it is not only the content of these everyday conversations that is perturbing, but also the matter-of-fact delivery—like college students discussing classwork. Any considerations of moral, ethical, social, or health issues were completely absent from these exchanges. Sentences that could hurl a feminist into a seething rage, bring a mother to tears, or reduce friends back home to pained, confused (and sometimes jealous) silence were standard fare at the Majestic. Just a few of the thousands of samples I have in my notes;

"Yeah, one time in Tool Kok, a bird grabbed my dick as I was walking past, so I just grabbed her tits and shoved my hand up her skirt. When she grabbed my arse with her other hand and started dragging me inside, I knew she'd be a good shag."

"That one was really young. No pussy hair at all. But it was weird, she had these little undeveloped tits with hair on her nipples."

"Sure I gave her a two-dollar tip. She was the best shag I've had in Cambodia. Excellent blowjob, and then we did it from behind. She moved her hips up and down, and I couldn't even stop her. I walked out of the cubicle shaking."

"She was pretty small, and I felt awkward being on top. I told her to go on top, but she didn't want to. I just laid there until she climbed up and got me off."

"Last time I went to Svay Pa I took two at the same time. I reckon they were about sixteen max. I had one of them suck the other's left tit while I sucked the right one. They wouldn't eat each other out though."

"She still hasn't forgiven me from the last time in the brothel. I kind of forced her to let me shag her up the ass. It must've hurt, but I gave her a nice tip."

"I think she might actually like me. From the first time I brought her home, she's been really into it. Kissing, blowjobs and everything. And then she even follows me into the shower to wash my dick and stuff. Great service, and I don't mind paying her a little extra for it."

"Just think about all the bullshit you have to go through to get laid back home. Wouldn't it be great if you could use the same line as here; you know, 'Here's five bucks, now get your clothes off and suck my dick.'"

With so many residents eager to initiate me, I soon learned about the four main flesh markets frequented by foreigners. Ranking the areas in some kind of descending order of 'classiness', we begin with Champagne. This renowned Phnom Penh institution has a dance floor, an open air movie theater with tables, two bars, three food stalls, and, of course, hundreds of girls. The proportion is about half each of Vietnamese and Khmer, and they range from quite young, perhaps as young as 15 or 16, to over 35. They go for the night for as low as $10, but a very attractive girl may be able to charge a 'rich' (read gullible) tourist $30 or $40. The differentiating factor about Champagne is that the girls come and go as they please, and are free to accept or refuse any offer at will. Joe, for example, avoids brothels, preferring, as he jokingly says, "The mystique of picking up a girl at a bar."

For the brothels, the 'classiest' of the three main areas is Svay Pa, a village 11 kilometers out of town that consists almost entirely of brothels. The girls here, almost exclusively Vietnamese, range in age from 14 to 25. One of the brothels, known as "Kiddie Corner" offers 12 and 13-year-olds. The girls in Svay Pa are 'hostesses' as well as prostitutes. Five dollars buys not only oral sex and then intercourse, but also a companion for the afternoon or evening. It is very common for guys to spend entire Sunday mornings or afternoons drinking beer with, and having sex with, their companion(s). The prostitutes can also be taken out for the night for $20 to $25.

Within the city are a couple of rows of brothels concentrated on Streets 154 and 63. The girls here are also almost entirely Vietnamese and the price is also $5. However, the facilities are not as 'upmarket' as in Svay Pa, and there is a less relaxed atmosphere. Because of the higher costs of being in the city, the brothels need a higher turnover of clients, so customers are not encouraged to lounge around with a hostess as at Svay Pa.

Last is Tool Kok. This is actually the name of an entire neighborhood in northern Phnom Penh, but when referred to by decadent foreigners, it signifies a three kilometer stretch of Street 70. Shack after wooden shack, lining both sides of the street, is filled with 13 to 25-year-old girls ready to drop their panties for $2—although foreigners often pay as much as $3 or $4. The facilities are minimal; tiny and filthy cardboard-partitioned cubicles with a bed inside. And the pace in Tool Kok is furious; an assembly line of prostitutes and customers—with, Joe jokes, "All the mystique of a napalm strike." This is the sex industry at its most industrial.

Within this sexually charged atmosphere, people have varying attitudes toward prostitution. It does not take long to find examples of men who have run amok here. Gary is an American, about six-foot-six and stocky, but not overweight. He has long, neatly groomed hair, but through no fault of his own, he is quite ugly. He is also the holder of a master's degree in History and has made a 'career' of traveling around the world having paid and unpaid sex. He is now on an extended vacation from Japan—where he has a good income from teaching, and a nice girlfriend. Although he looks about 35, he is actually 52.

Every single conversation I or anyone else has ever had with Gary revolves around sex. The only exceptions are when I point blank ask him a question regarding some other topic. Otherwise, the topic is always sex, and usually brothels. The man is an unstoppable machine, spending whole days at Svay Pa, or prowling Tool Kok in the mornings and then going to Champagne at night. Whatever his psychological framework was before he arrived in Cambodia, his present motivations are movingly simple; Gary wants to ejaculate into as many different human females as time and stamina permit—and in Cambodia he can partake of this all-you-can eat buffet of female flesh for less than many Americans spend on their car each month.

We once worked out a potential monthly sex budget for Gary and took wildly optimistic stamina figures just to ascertain the most extreme result; if Gary, every day of his life, has sex with two girls in Svay Pa at $6 each (including tip), and two girls in Tool Kok at $3 each (including tip), plus one girl from Champagne each weekend night at a generous $20, he will be spending a total of $700 a month on sex. Not a bad deal considering that it entitles him to 128 different women in thirty days. Gary discusses his pastime with all the sincerity and genuine excitement one might find, say, in a grandfather showing his lifelong baseball card collection to his enthusiastic grandson.

For many, this atmosphere of complete openness is actually one of the main attractions of Cambodian prostitution. I arrive at the Majestic one day to hear Will, a 45-year-old beach bum from Hawaii, speaking uncharacteristically loudly to the others at the table. "They already fucked up the rest of the world. Why can't they just leave Cambodia alone? It was a little corner where they didn't have control, and now they've come to take over here as well." For such a mellow guy, Will is quite upset. "They're gonna ruin it for everyone. They already screwed up Thailand, and now they're gonna screw up Cambodia."

Fearing for the future of this fragile country, I inquire about the disaster. Will responds by giving me an article from *The Cambodia Daily*. The piece describes a raid on "Kiddie Corner," the one brothel in Svay Pa notorious for providing very young prostitutes to its clients. Three 13-year-olds and one 12-year-old were rescued from the brothel, while unknown others slipped out the back. The raid was organized with help from ECPAT (End Child Prostitution in Asia Today), and the police taking part were told of the destination only minutes before they arrived so that they would not be able to warn the brothel as usually happens. Will goes on indignantly; "First they go after child prostitution, but they won't be satisfied with that. You can't appease these people. They'll be after everyone else soon enough. Don't underestimate what they can do. They throw all this money around, and before you know it, everything we like about Cambodia will be gone. They're out for blood, and they don't care about the consequences of their actions."

Another teacher consoles him; "But you can still go to Svay Pa and get a shag. That won't change."

But Will is not mollified. "Even if you can still sneak in for a shag . . . ," he frowns and shakes his head, "I mean, part of the fun was walking down the street and seeing all the girls outside, and them waving at you and hugging you as you come by—the whole fun atmosphere. If I have to sneak in and out like some criminal, who needs it?"

If you met Will in the US, he would strike you as a perfectly normal guy. It would be very difficult to imagine him complaining so bitterly about an operation designed to prevent 12 and 13-years-olds from selling their bodies. But at least Gary and Will, unlike others, are not themselves attracted to the very youngest of the prostitutes available. Steve tells me how, because of Eric's preferences, his housemates had to institute a rule at their house; no prostitutes 14 or younger back to the house (sex with 14-year-olds anywhere else was not addressed). One day, I sit with Eric after he returned from a trip to Svay Pa that left him smiling broadly. I ask him about his encounter and he wastes no time launching into the vivid description; "It was wonderful. I went down on this girl before we shagged. I love eating out a girl so young that she has no pussy hair," he says with a lascivious smile. "She must've liked it because after we shagged and showered, I sat on the bed watching her get dressed. She stopped and looked at me. Then she pulled off her panties and got on the bed and pushed her pussy in my face. I was happy to oblige, I promise you."

I try, and fail, to imagine another situation in which a group of men would sit in a public restaurant and loudly discuss the purchase of sex from barely pubescent females. While I am still getting accustomed to it, the group at the Majestic has long been inured to Eric's explicit tales of fucking young girls. Even his announcement one day of, "I had a wonderful class today. I had a very sexy ten-year-old girl suck my finger," elicits no raised eyebrows, merely statements of envy and urgent requests for details. He is more than happy to oblige; "Well, in class, this girl was talking with her friend, so I walked over and pointed at her to stop. The depraved little bitch grabs my finger with her mouth. I just stood there and let her suck. Eventually she let go but after that I couldn't concentrate on teaching, I promise you. I ran to a brothel right after class and had the quickest orgasm ever. She must have sucked my finger for at least a minute." There is silence at the table as each man present savors the image in his own way.

Even though Gary's enthusiasm and Eric's predilections evoke no outrage at the Majestic, most of the residents take a more 'moderate' view of paying impoverished girls for sexual release. The majority of the group simply sees the brothels and Champagne as just one of the many hedonistic diversions that Phnom Penh has to offer. An evening out can consist of a movie, a game of snooker, a beer in a bar, getting stoned by the river, or sex in a brothel; none more exciting or scandalous than the others.

Even those with moral or ethical reservations about the brothels usually end up paying for sex in Cambodia. In a country with such strong cultural sanctions against sex before marriage (for girls), having any kind of companionship at all usually involves an exchange of cash. The line separating prostitution from 'normal' relationships is blurred in the sense that a boyfriend with means is fully expected to support his girlfriend. Joe, for example, disapproves of the brothels—especially the under-18 prostitutes, but he brings home girls from Champagne hoping eventually to forge a relationship with one of them.

Joe's resigned acceptance of behavior he does not condone is similar to the attitudes I glean from many of the women expats in Cambodia. Evelyn is an easygoing Englishwoman with an upper-class accent and a friendly nature. Cambodia is an extended work-stop on her long tour through India and Southeast Asia. While her presence at the table is sometimes enough to stifle the most explicit details, the guys hardly conceal their activities for her benefit. She describes how she handles it; "At first I was pretty disgusted and depressed about it, but since I got here I've mellowed about some things at least. I accept that it's an ugly reality of life here, and until I can change it, that's the way it'll stay. I wish there was another way. But the thing is, I could never support these girls myself, so who am I to say that what they're doing to earn money is wrong unless I can give them an alternative. But that still doesn't make it right for a family to sell their daughter for a TV set, or a second motorbike—and that happens far too often.

"At least most of the guys I hang out with aren't abusive. That really makes me mad, when you see guys who can't even get a date in their home countries come here and start treating women like shit because here, all of a sudden, they can get away with it. I know you can hire hit men in Cambodia, but I've often wondered if you can hire 'hit castrators.' But the guys that are my friends are not like that and I appreciate it. Sure, I find plenty of the things they do despicable. But I often see them honestly affectionate with the girls and sometimes, not often, but sometimes, the girls really like them back.

"But still, even if they're decent to the girls, I can see how it affects their views on women. Even in the best circumstances, say back home in Barclays Bank or Oxford University, it's so easy for men to treat women as objects. So when women's bodies are on sale for two dollars a go, it's pretty damn tough. Sometimes I see guys looking at me, and they have to remind themselves there's more to women than just rented bodies. And you know, I feel sorry for the girls who have to go through this to support their parents or their kids. And it bothers me to see guys here who you know wouldn't act this way at home. Yeah, so prostitution is an accepted part of Khmer society, but that doesn't mean they don't know there's something wrong with all this. They pretend to have just woken up in Cambodia and not have any idea that people back home would be disgusted.

"But the one thing that bothers me more than anything is the children. I mean, with so many girls seventeen or eighteen and older available, there's just no excuse for having sex with a fourteen-year-old. They belong in school, not in a brothel. I think of these pubescent girls being jumped on by five or ten men a day, and it breaks my heart. And when guys I know do that, it really pisses me off. But I think what's most tragic is that so many of these girls have so little to look forward to. Unless there's some miracle cure, a lot of them will die of AIDS before they turn twenty-five."

Evelyn hits on a very pertinent point here. The desperate AIDS situation in Cambodia is not only confined to prostitutes and to Khmer men who are ignorant of, or unconcerned about, HIV infection. One would expect that educated Westerners, even in Phnom Penh, would exercise caution in their activities with prostitutes. But the same Cambodian environment that enables many inside it to shed their inhibitions against buying sex from young girls, also seems to make them lose their instinct for self-preservation as well. With all the time spent discussing sex with prostitutes, one might imagine that plenty of time would also be devoted to the subject of safe sex and AIDS prevention. However, in a perversity typical of Cambodia, discussions on safe sex and HIV were shockingly low in both frequency and quality. This is especially distressing given the extent of the AIDS crisis in Cambodia. Experts estimate that 50% of the sex workers in Cambodia are HIV-positive, although I was never able to reveal the methodology or reliability behind this statistic. Unofficially, a worker at Cambodia's Pasteur Institute, which provides free HIV testing, reported that about 15% of the people coming for the tests test positive. Because this is a self-selecting group, it is not clear how representative this is of either the general or the sex worker populations.

It is clear, however, that HIV and AIDS are widespread and growing problems. Cambodia is considered to have the most rapid infection rate in the world, and efforts at AIDS education and prevention are woefully inadequate. A common myth among Khmer men is that taking antibiotics before going to a brothel is an appropriate HIV prophylactic. The uphill battle against AIDS is reflected in the words of one prostitute quoted in a newspaper; "I'd rather die of AIDS next year than of starvation tomorrow." If present trends continue, Cambodia could face an AIDS-induced genocide more destructive than even Pol Pot's insane reign of terror.

In this context, the general lack of concern among foreigners at the Majestic is even more mind-boggling. The longest discussion I ever heard about condoms was hardly a testimony to safe sex. The participants began by talking about the aid-subsidized 'Number 1' condom brand, which is the most common condom in the brothels. They also have a tendency to break. One teacher notes that; "Yeah, I'd say they break on me about a third of the time." Reiner joins in, asking, "And you pull out, right?" but quickly answers himself, "Wrong! Come on. I mean even with a condom, shagging these girls is wonderful, but the condom breaks and it's the greatest feeling in the world. I mean, I know we're supposed to pull out, but after it breaks it's only a couple of seconds 'til I come anyway. My brain says, 'Condom break! Pull out! Pull out!' But my brain's lost control, and of course I don't pull out. And you know what? I just pump even harder until I have that great no-condom orgasm."

"Speaking of which," contributes another teacher, "that brothel in TK [Tool Kok] last night was bad news. Remember how we went in right after that huge group of Khmers came out. I was shagging this bird, and she was really creamed up. I must've been sloshing around after those bareback riders had greased her up. They looked like they really enjoyed themselves, didn't they. There's not much worse than sloppy seconds, but at least she was wet. Usually they're as dry as a bone."

But at least the guys in this conversation use condoms. This is not a given among the decadent expat crowd. Joe tells me about Hal; "He was incredible. 'Hey Hal, how's it going?'" Joe imitates Hal by adopting a low, spaced-out tone; "'Well, there's this white stuff coming out of my dick. Must be from the girl in TK last week.'" In his own voice, Joe recreates the obvious next question; "You didn't use a condom?" Back to Hal's brain-dead monotone; "'No way, man. The latex industry pollutes, and it's totally exploitative, man. I won't support the latex industry at all.'" I beg Joe to tell me he is joking. I am almost frantic to be reassured that, even in Cambodia, such incredible stupidity is only mythical. "No, those were his words. 'I won't support the latex industry.' Anyway, he went home to England with AIDS, but not before shagging this girl at Champagne for a couple of months. The last time I saw her there, she showed me his address and told me he'll come back for her and that she misses him, and how he's working in England for the two of them, and how she knows it's true even though she hasn't received any letters. I can't believe it. She's deeply in love with the fucker who gave her AIDS and then left her to sell her body to support herself. Sometimes this place is just too depressing."

This conversation with Joe helps prepare me for a discussion with Jean, a Frenchman living off French unemployment benefits. Joining us one day at the Majestic, Jean begins speaking eloquently of the beauty of having paid sex without a condom. It makes all the difference between "just a shag and a true sexual experience." It also increases his stamina; "This one brothel had six girls in it. I just stayed there all afternoon until I'd shagged them all. Wearing a condom, I'd never have gotten past number three or four."

Jean is aware of STDs, but maintains, "They're all curable, except for HIV which is impossible for a healthy man to catch from a woman." And in logic that can only come from an expat in Cambodia, he tells us that, "I'm safe anyway because I get tested every three months and they've all come out negative."

A man who was not so lucky shows up at the Majestic during my second trip. I am sitting alone, going over my notes from the afternoon, when I see a slightly pudgy, bald, middle-aged foreigner march into the restaurant and greet the assembled. From the salutations, it is easy for me to catch that his name is Herve. He used to live in Cambodia and is now returning after a long absence. Eavesdropping halfheartedly on the reunion, I hear the same word over and over again; "... AIDS ... AIDS ..." Putting down my notes, I pay full attention as Herve speaks to the crowd. "Yeah, didn't you know I have AIDS? I'm on treatment now, and maybe it'll save my life. All these little pills here. I hate taking them, I mean they do awful things to your body. It's basically that I'm eating poison, but it's better these little poison pills than AIDS. I take two of these in the morning, and then this one and this one at noon, and then another two of the first one along with this one in the evening. And each pill costs about a dollar, but the government pays for most of it. And I feel sick and nauseous all the time. If only I was younger. But my body was tired even before I started the treatment, so putting this poison in my body is just shit. The doctors explain it this way; your immune system is a train track and the virus is the train. When the train reaches the end of the track, that's it, you die. The drugs slow the train down and allow my body to build more track. Hopefully I'll have time to build some more track before the train reaches the end. But it's not a cure for AIDS, what happens is that it kills the virus down to undetectable levels. But you can never shag without a condom again."

The guys have started to shift uncomfortably now. Herve has dampened the mood for the planned whoring expedition. They were happy to see him, but did not want their dinner turned into a lecture on HIV infection, and especially not from someone so seemingly eager to let the world know about his HIV status. People start filtering out; once they get inside a brothel with a beer in their hands and a 15-year-old on their laps, the mood will return. As the last of the regulars make their exit, I invite Herve to join me so that he will not have to eat dinner alone in a restaurant full of strangers to whom he has just announced that he is dying of AIDS.

One of the first guys to leave Herve's lecture to head for Tool Kok is a brothel enthusiast named Henrik. Some readers will dismiss and condemn all brothel patrons as evil sexual predators who take advantage of poverty to control women.

But Henrik's case shows that not all men's motivations are so clear cut. Henrik is tall, intelligent, and attractive, with thick longish black hair and an easy smile. He comes from a well-off family in Denmark and tells me about himself in almost perfect English. "I wish I was born early enough to have fought in the Viet Nam War. I'd definitely have volunteered. I can't think of anything more exciting than slogging through the jungle like that. It must've been great." All this is said with the most innocent grin and twinkling eyes you can imagine. The killing of others and the danger of being killed do not seem to even enter the equation. Henrik, unlike most urban Danes, eagerly looked forward to the draft process, and was crushed when a minor heart problem kept him out of the army. He is the perfect example of a schoolboy naively romanticizing the horror of war.

"As soon as I finished university in Denmark I started spending all my time in Christiania [an 'alternative lifestyle' community in Copenhagen where drugs are freely available]. I was getting sucked in, but at least I could see it, so I left to visit Viet Nam. Anyway, who wants to live in a country where they don't allow the army to shoot weapons," he says, referring to recent Danish legislation prohibiting the army from firing live ammunition. "On the way I stopped here. I really liked it, so I stayed. But I had to leave because I was addicted to the brothels. I was every night in a brothel. Often two per one day. It was getting so that I couldn't concentrate until I'd shagged. And I was getting into all these fantasies, too. You know, American GI on R and R. So I went to Viet Nam to chill out. It's really hard to shag there. There's always something dodgy with the police, and the prostitutes picking your pockets and stuff. Mostly I go out into the jungle, into the old battlefields from the war, and masturbate. But I'm back now, and ready for front-line duty. You know, shagging in the brothels, combat."

Henrik not only romanticizes war, he equates it with having sex with prostitutes. Like almost everything else in Cambodia, the residents at the Majestic ignore the chilling implications of this analogy and are merely amused. One lunch conversation focuses specifically on developing this brothel/combat analogy. The brothels are the "front lines," and going shagging is going "into combat" or being in a "firefight." Spending a lot of time in a brothel (or brothels) is "heavy combat." Henrik and Steve's recent "expedition eleven clicks north" was the "Battle of Svay Pa." Steve, who took two girls into the cubicle, announces that, "I fought the Battle of Svay Pa on two fronts."

For the troops, there are ranks based on "combat experience" and ability. Big Gary is the perfect sergeant; a relentless trooper who slogs his way through combat day after day without showing any fatigue. But he lacks the creativity and initiative to become an officer. Hawaiian Will is a great first lieutenant; he is a pro at what he does, and you can always count on him in a firefight. Henrik was the commander for a while, but Steve's heavy combat experience of late may force Henrik to turn over command to him.

If the condom breaks during combat, that is "taking casualties," and the wounded trooper is entitled to a "Purple Dick." This is not only a play on Purple Heart, but an unfortunately apt description of the potential result of "taking casualties." They give code names to the different brothel areas; Street 154 is "Fire Base Alpha," Tool Kok is "Fire Base Bravo," and Svay Pa is "Fire Base Charlie."

Just as he romanticizes war, Henrik romanticizes the brothel girls. It is truly touching to hear him describe his quest for love—one $5 fuck at a time. One Sunday morning, I am at the Majestic with Jeff—an enthusiastic newcomer to Cambodia currently being initiated by the veterans—when Henrik shows up with a huge grin and says, "Glad you're here. I'm recruiting volunteers for action on the front lines." He makes noises imitating the boom of artillery shells landing. "Are you ready for combat duty?"

Jeff practically stands at attention. "Which front's gonna see action today, Commander?"

"Fire Base Charlie could see some fierce firefights." Jeff looks confused, so Henrik elaborates; "Fire Base Charlie is our forward defense base. You know," more artillery noises from Henrik, "deep inside enemy territory."

"Eleven kilometers deep?"

"That's right soldier."

Jeff agrees to be ready "to deploy" in half an hour.

I get the "debriefing" from Jeff later that evening. "Henrik wanted me to drive so he could concentrate on his 'tactical planning.' Once we arrived at Fire Base Charlie, Henrik directed me to the LZ [Landing Zone, i.e. brothel]. As soon as we went in, Henrik found the girl he'd come for, and it was just like two old friends."

"I picked my girl and we went upstairs. It was cool to watch Henrik in action. He doesn't speak much Vietnamese but they managed to have a real conversation. Henrik was with her two weeks ago, but it was almost like an older brother looking after his kid sister."

Well, not exactly like that; Henrik and his girl went off for their first round, as did Jeff and his partner. With this comes a long explanation of what a wonderful shag Jeff had because he instructed his girl to keep her boots on during the whole session. He continues; "We hung out on the sofa until Henrik and his chick came back. They were still flirting, like they'd just gone out for a coffee instead of a shag. Watching Henrik is really weird. He was flirting and touching her, but real sweet you know, not the usual groping she's used to. He's romantic, like almost innocent. After we all shagged again, we figured we'd done our part for the war effort, and could return to HQ with pride."

Henrik is happy to satisfy my curiosity about his attitude. "Most of these girls are really wonderful. They're just great girls. I love to be near them, to talk with them, just to be with them. They're so fresh, and so fun. I guess I get attached to them too much, but I can't help it. They're just so lovely." He gets a bit defensive when I ask if he would be so enthusiastic if there were no sex, or at least no guaranteed sex. "I'd still love them, and think they're great girls, but now the blowjobs and the shagging are so normal that I'd really miss it."

Clearly, Henrik does not go to brothels because he hates women or because he wants to control them. He feels genuine affection for the girls he pays to sleep with, and, regardless of how one judges his expression of it, a fondness for women in general. Certainly in the world of paid sex, a romantic is bound to be disappointed. With a mixture of anger and humor, he tells me of an experience in Bo Din, a brothel area very similar to Tool Kok, but on a smaller scale. "I'd already had a shag that afternoon, but I was still horny so I walked over to Bo Din to find that fifteen-year-old Khmer girl I had last week. I just about reach her brothel when my dick gets grabbed through my pants by this Vietnamese girl. She says two dollars, none of the usual haggling. Hey, even though she's not that pretty, there's no way I can resist such a bargain shag.

"Anyway, she takes off her clothes and then helps me undress. And she gives me a very decent blowjob without the usual rush. She slips a condom on me and then moves on top. Usually these girls never agree do any of that unless you tell them but she lies on top of me and it's like we're actually making love. She really seems to be into it. Then she says, 'Let's take the condom off so I can have your baby.'

"About then, I noticed she's getting dry, so I reached for the K-Y Jelly I keep in my pocket. But I don't see my pants, and the girl has this funny look on her face. Then I see my pants being pushed into the cubicle through the space under the partition. So that's what was going on with this wonderful shag. I got my wallet and counted the money and saw right away that some fucker took out a twenty dollar bill.

"I won't give in quietly so I started banging on the partition yelling in Vietnamese that I want my money back. I open the door and keep banging and yelling. The other girls came out into the hallway but the mamasan told them to get back to work. They must've been freaked looking at me, this tall, bony guy wearing nothing but glasses and a condom on his limp dick. Of course, they all play innocent, including the bitch who fucked me.

"Anyway, I kept yelling 'Where's my money?' and I was making a good stand in my condom and glasses. They told me to put my clothes on, but fuck that. If I got dressed they'd throw me out in the street, but they wouldn't if I was naked.

Eventually they give the money back but they still won't admit they took it. The mamasan pisses off and I go back in to the girl.

"I tell you, she was really shocked when I told her I wanted to finish shagging. All the affection was gone. For the past twenty minutes I'd been barely under control but now I'm telling her to finish the job. It was really weird to shag someone I was so angry at. I didn't really like it but, hey, I was proud that I only used one condom for both times."

By my April trip to Phnom Penh, Henrik has finally found his brothel love. I run into him outside the Majestic, and he is giddy with delight. "This is Nga," he says proudly, introducing her as if showing off his brand new sports car. "She's usually booked solid, but I went to her brothel at the right time today. I've been waiting ages to take her out for the night."

By my July trip, Henrik and Nga are living together and Henrik is talking about marriage. While Joe respects their love for each other, the circumstances of their meeting are irresistible grist for his satire. Joe jokes about Henrik and Nga telling their grandchildren how they met. "Henrik would start off; 'I looked across the crowded brothel, and among all the girls in hot pants and sleazy dresses, one stood out. It was magic, and I knew that as long as they didn't try to charge me more than five dollars, this was the girl for me. I took her in my arms that moment, and we went upstairs to shag ourselves senseless.' And then Nga joins in; 'Of all the seven guys I fucked that day, your grandfather was definitely my favorite. I didn't even mind when he didn't tip me. And do you know what? The next time he came to the brothel, I knew as soon as I went down to suck his dick that he had washed and cleaned it especially for me.' Henrik again; 'Yes, kids, we were both pretty shy back then. For the next month, I kept quiet while she was humped by Chinese businessmen, Khmer generals, and most of my friends. But I knew that true love would win out.' And then Nga; 'Your grandfather's right. I knew that he'd come back, and not just for a quick shag. And here we are, living happily ever after.'"

Joe's satire aside, the fact is that Henrik and Nga are a handsome couple who have developed a strong and caring relationship.

Svay Pa Brothel Village
July 10, 1997

The constant talk of sex with nubile young women for paltry amounts of money has my curiosity piqued in more than just a journalistic sense. Rationalization or not, I believe that the book requires at least some 'field research' on this topic. As I ponder the question, I also realize that part of the reason I resist going to the brothels is my fear that I will enjoy it too much. In the end, I delayed my 'investigations' until (what I expected to be) my last trip to Cambodia.

On this bright Sunday morning, a couple of the guys meet at the Majestic to fuel up before an expedition to Svay Pa. After two more rationalizations, I ask to join them. First of all, I will only buy oral sex, as if that is somehow less culpable than full intercourse. This will also mean that I will be at an extremely low risk for HIV transmission. Also, pathetically, I justify to myself that I should be getting some exercise, and 11 km each way is a good distance for a bike ride. They zoom off, and I set out to rent a bicycle to join them.

Today is a typical Cambodian summer morning; cloudless, sunny, and heating up fast. The road takes me north up the river past the Japanese Bridge and out of the city. It's semi-rural here; wooden houses instead of concrete, and small shops and workshops instead of large shophouse restaurants and stores. There are shops on the main road, but only fields behind them. I pass a few Cham (Cambodian Muslim) mosques. As the surroundings get increasingly rural, I start to wonder if I have missed the exit off the 'highway.'

Upon reaching the unmistakable landmark of "the big pink factory," I know I have arrived. This is it. Svay Pa. Kilometer number 11 on the 'highway.' I turn off and follow the dirt road down a steep hill, then take a left past the hotel, and then

Beauty and the beast. Street No. 63, downtown Phnom Penh.

The Royal Palace, Phnom Penh.

Monuments on Sihanouk Boulevard. From foreground to background—fountains in the forms of a lotus flower and five-headed naga, and the Independence Monument.

Riverside at Sisowath Quay.

Royaume du Cambodge

Canton, le 30 Décembre 1973

Monsieur,

J'ai l'honneur de vous faire connaître que
le Prince Méthavi est indigné de votre idée de
proposer comme premier ministre U SAY, partisan de
Lou Nol, tous traitres à la nation khmère.

Je vous rappelle les termes de mon dernier
télégramme :" SON ALTESSE ROYALE LE PRINCE NORODOM
SIHANOUK N'ACCEPTE AUCUN COMPROMIS OU NEGOCIATIONS
AVEC LA CLIQUE DE LON NOL".

Veuillez agréer, Monsieur, l'expression de
mes sentiments distingués.

LE DIRECTEUR DE CABINET,

PUNG PENG CHENG

sieur M. HENN
tern EXXDIFINANCE
BOX 967
ntiaine
L O S

Document from the files of Dr. Max Henn showing that Prince
Sihanouk refused to consider the possibility of negotiations with Loon
Nol and the Khmer Republican leadership that might have ended
the civil war in 1973.

Police and onlookers gather at the scene of a drug shoot-out on Sihanouk boulevard.

The aftermath of the shoot-out in an alley behind the building. The victim was an alleged amphetamine dealer.

Ganja (and other assorted dry goods) stall at Tool Tom Poong (Russian Market). Unidentified animal skins hang splayed on sticks above the main display.

Score! $2 bag of ganja bought at the same stall.

Civilians fleeing Phnom Penh on Monivong Boulevard as smoke rises from fighting near the airport during the July 1997 coup.

Jubilant soldiers drive by on Mao Tse Tung Boulevard with refrigerators and other appliances looted from civilians. The victims look on powerless to react.

Thai commandos evacuating Thai nationals during the July 1997 coup. Pochentong International Airport.

Battle damage to the terminal building as a result of the coup. Pochentong International Airport.

Burned-out tank on Pochentong boulevard after the coup.

Another completely destroyed tank on Pochentong Boulevard. The turret lies out of shot on the ground next to the main body of the vehicle.

immediately turn right. The sight that greets me is absolutely unbelievable. On both sides of the unpaved road through the middle of the village are brothels. Nothing but brothels. And of course, flaunting themselves provocatively outside each one, girls; young, beautiful Vietnamese girls in tight shorts or evening gowns, and all of them beckoning with, "You, you, go sleep, go boom-boom!"

It feels like some surreal Western as I slowly make my way down the center of 'Main Street.' The dusty street running through the middle of a one-horse town; the lone traveler squinting in the harsh sun; the lovely hookers, out of place in the middle of the wilderness. The girls are all on display in the formations that their mamasans have arranged—a kind of whore inspection line for the passing customers. As I ride down the road, most wave at me or call, "You, you." The more brazen girls break formation and come out to grab me or block my path. There are hundreds of girls outside the brothels and countless others inside—a true fairyland of prostitution.

When I finally find the motorbikes, I set my bicycle next to them, enter the establishment, and go upstairs to find Eric, Steve, and Henrik. They explain the Svay Pa brothel layout. Like the brothels within Phnom Penh, they have a main reception area—where the girls can be inspected and selected— and small rooms for getting down to business. The rooms tend to be more spacious and more 'luxurious' than even the 'upmarket' $5 brothels in town, and certainly more than the $2 brothels. But the really delightful part, they tell me enthusiastically, are the 'lounges'—small areas partitioned with curtains that contain two couches and a little table in the middle. In these cozy nooks, you can spend time with your girl before and/or after the shag(s), get to know her, share a beer or some fertilized duck eggs (that contain almost fully developed embryos), joke around, have a few laughs, and just basically hang out with your friends and a group of lovely, obliging young women.

The guys have all had sex once already today, and are now precisely in that mode of hanging out in the intimate lounge area. They introduce me to the girls and give ratings on their

103

sexual abilities. With my curiosity and excitement growing, I find an attractive girl who looks about 19. With my limited Vietnamese, and a series of humiliating (for me at least, if not also for her) hand gestures, I make my requirements known. She consents (whatever that means in this place) and, after I shower to clean up from the bike ride, she leads me to a small room. The experience is most memorable for the incredible beauty of the face and body of this young woman. It is also memorable for the complete lack of passion or excitement or pleasure on her part. I start thinking about my last haircut. The barber was also a young Vietnamese woman, and we chatted pleasantly, even flirted, as she cut my hair. I realize that my haircut was an infinitely more romantic and sensual experience than this present one.

I look at the girl. Whatever sense of social justice I possess feels sadness at her fate. But the visceral part of me responds with uncaring gratification at the privilege it allows me. She looks up, slightly embarrassed that I am watching. I smile at her, and she smiles back sweetly before going back to her chore. Even as I wonder if there is no other way that this pleasant young woman can earn a living for her family, I know that the $3 she will earn for this 15 minute procedure ($2 goes to the house) is more than her rice-farming parents earn in a day. Should I blame the brutal American war effort, or the idiocy of Marxist economics? The punishing embargo that followed America's defeat? Or Viet Nam's own expensive and expansionist invasion of Cambodia? Or should I place the blame on my own silent acquiescence as I sit and listen to the conversations at the Majestic? The thoughts fade as male biology takes over.

Soon, my 'date' and I join the group in the lounge area. This is Svay Pa at its best; it's a sunny day, and I'm with three friends drinking beer, joking, and relaxing. That is usually enough for a really great day. But here in Cambodia, there is a bonus. We are accompanied by four nubile young women who are waiting to oblige us with their bodies as often as our stamina and wallets allow. In the meantime, they are there only to please us with their smiles and company. Not only that, but a whole group of equally obliging young girls are waiting downstairs, willing to replace or join any of the girls with us already. Admittedly, these illiterate farm girls, who cannot speak a word of English, do not provide the most scintillating intellectual conversation. But with a beautiful 17-year-old sitting on his lap hoping that she can make some extra cash by fucking him, any male can easily make do with intellectual shallowness for an afternoon. With each beer and each look at these lovely young women, I can feel myself getting drawn into this world. I wonder just how far gone I am already.

Once all the other couples have gone off for their second rounds of fucking, we call for the bill. For 7 'times', 12 beers, 4 sodas, 2 coconuts, and 10 fertilized duck eggs, the total bill for the four of us is $53. What an incredible feeling as we head out of the brothel together. We feel like powerful, conquering heroes; the liberators of Paris and the city has offered up all its young maidens (so to speak) for the taking. Or maybe we're rock stars, surrounded by 500 groupies. Or we're James Bond or Don Juan, jumping from girl to beautiful girl. We're Kings of Arabia with a harem of girls for the taking. At $5 a girl it doesn't take much to buy a lot of pleasure or fantasy in Svay Pa.

As the other guys roar off on their motorbikes, I am thankful for the solitary bike ride home and the thinking space it allows me. Have I just used, in the fullest sense of the word, a young girl forced by poverty or worse, to submit to my sexual whims? Or have I helped some family of subsistence farmers somewhere in southern Viet Nam make it through the month? Did I just expose myself and any future lovers to death from AIDS? Have I just committed a moral outrage, or am I merely the latest customer of the world's oldest profession? I also wonder at how many trips to Svay Pa it would take before these questions stopped mattering to me. The truth is, I now have a much clearer understanding of these guys' attachment to Cambodia. If you don't have too many moral inhibitions or achievement ambitions, Svay Pa is the perfect place to waste a few years of your life.

The Edge
July 11, 1997

I am ready to take another research trip, this time to Tool Kok. My plan, and my rationalizations, are identical to the Svay Pa trip. Steve and Eric need precious little convincing to take me. Heading out of the Majestic, we turn left (north) onto Monivong. Shortly after the road to the lakefront, we come to an immense traffic circle. Three-quarters of the way around the circle, we exit. We are now on Street 70 or, as some French guide books refer to it, the Street of Young Flowers.

After passing the FUNCINPEC HQ and a brief stretch of undeveloped land, it begins; Shack after shack, wooden and dilapidated, stretching off into the distance. Each has its pink fluorescent light and each has its bevy of young girls cajoling or demanding that passing men enter for sex. We drive by slowly, and witness an uninterrupted orgy of prostitution lining the potholed, rutted road as far as we can see. We are pulled and grabbed and shoved by girls eager to get us inside. Sex is a numbers game here; at $2–$3 per fuck, these girls have to go through a tremendous number of men to earn enough to send home to their families and/or pay off their debts.

I feel awed by the sheer magnitude of the scene. As we cruise up the street and then back down, I am simply dizzy off the atmosphere. These thousands of girls looking to have sex for a couple of dollars create an energy that goes beyond anything I have ever seen before. While I am awed by the enormity of the spectacle, Steve and Eric are ready to fuck.

We turn into one of the brothels—how they picked this one out of the hundreds of choices is beyond me. The wooden floor sags perceptibly under the weight of the motorcycles, but it holds. They want $4 because we are foreigners. We know the price is $2, but settle on $3, conceding that it is still a pretty good deal. I am led into the cubicle by an eager young Vietnamese girl. I had no idea how luxurious the rooms in Svay Pa are. These cubicles are really just partitions with cardboard or thin plyboard in between, and are barely big enough to undress in without standing on the bed. But undress we do, and I am again bowled over by the sight of a beautiful young girl's stunning body.

I look at the girl and I want to fuck her. Things are making sense in a different way than they did outside the brothel. I wonder if this is where I lose it. I wonder if this is where I break with the past, and enter a new world with different rules. Can 28 years of perspective be undone by this 16-year-old's firm, available body? Is it really this easy for my way of thinking to shift? If I let go and enter this world where fucking 16-year-old girls for $3 is acceptable, where will it end? Can I try it just this once? Or will I be losing something forever, something more precious and more powerful than the animal urge pulling me toward the defenseless teenager on the bed? The battle goes on in my head as this confused Vietnamese girl is wondering what the problem is. Fortunately, some pissed up Khmer makes it easy for me by vomiting in the cubicle next door. We can't see or smell it, but the noise is very clear. In my mind, I turn my back on the squalor of this Tool Kok fuckhouse and head firmly back into the outside world. But physically, I am still in this room with a 16-year-old whore who is waiting for me to use her body. I pull out $5 and hand it to the confused girl, who is concerned that she has done something wrong and will be scolded, or worse, by the brothel owner. In Vietnamese, I explain, "You very good. I tired, I go home. I talk mamasan no problem." She seems to accept it, and thanks me for paying her without fucking her. She is getting dressed as I walk out of the cubicle to wait for Steve and Eric. I have enough perspective to fear that I do not have enough perspective, and commit to no further 'research' on this topic.

Drugs

> **"It's a good thing I had some
> smack left, or I never would've
> been able to stay awake for
> that second class."**

The fascination I found in Cambodia's perverse atmosphere made simply living in Phnom Penh a mind-altering, addictive intoxicant. But there were plenty of other stimulants available to assist the Phnom Penh residents in 'getting off' on their environment. Although the casual use of cheap, easily available drugs in Cambodia seems tame in comparison to the casual use of cheap, easily available women, drug use is flagrantly and openly celebrated by a large section of the expat community. As with Phnom Penh's other main vice, mind-altering chemicals are easily affordable and convenient to purchase. This, combined with the fact that taking drugs rarely hinders one's success in the English teaching career ladder, means that they play a large part in Phnom Penh's magic formula of easy girls, easy drugs, and easy work.

Until April of 1997, consumption of marijuana was not even illegal. It was, and still is, available in markets, and at incredibly cheap prices—usually $20 a kilogram. Heroin, however, is actually illegal, and so is not sold or consumed in public places. But it is still very cheap and easily available, and I never heard of an individual user having any hassles with either dealers or the police. Not only is the price—at $50 a gram—a fraction of the cost abroad, but the purity of the powder itself is almost 100%; much higher than the cut junk usually sold in the US.

The cheap drug bazaar does not stop with just regionally grown products. Phnom Penh's pharmacies are as well-stocked as they are loosely regulated. Prescriptions are unknown, and a wide range of amphetamines and barbiturates—regulated or illegal in the West—are sold inexpensively, openly, and legally across the counter in Phnom Penh. Finally, and most expensively, drugs such as Ecstasy and LSD are smuggled into Cambodia and sold at prices comparable to European levels.

Illicit drug use among Khmers is not a major concern. Mr. Rith, a Khmer journalist, explains that, "*Gaan-chah* grows very easily on the fields by the river. The farmers can just scatter the seeds and let it grow; they don't need to take care of it. Old men smoke it, but young people see it as purely an 'old man's habit.' Also, some people have the custom of eating it in chicken soup in the morning. But this is a very small amount, and the Ministry of Health doesn't see any problem with this." With its stigma as an old-fashioned, old men's drug, Cambodians looking for a high are much more likely to drink alcohol, or to get involved in such glamorous imported drugs like amphetamines or Ecstasy. These drugs are the focus of police crackdowns and enforcement, because it is these drugs, not marijuana, which pose a threat to Cambodian youth.

But the biggest 'drug problem' facing Cambodia today is tobacco. Spending millions of dollars in this small and impoverished country, the giant tobacco companies utilize advertising, concert promotions, lotteries, and direct sales in an all-out effort to hook Cambodians on their brands of cigarettes. Besides tobacco, the other main drug concern among the general population is that Khmers are pill-happy; the slightest head cold is cause for a trip to the pharmacy and the purchase of a full cocktail of various pills.

While marijuana use among Khmers is limited to old men and chicken soup, foreigners show no such restraint. Lighting up a joint at the Majestic is about as noteworthy as opening a can of soda. Upstairs on the guesthouse porch, there is almost always community ganja lying on the porch table. Steve explains; "Weed is so cheap that it doesn't make sense to be possessive. We just leave some on the table to save people the trouble of going to their rooms to get their stash." He waves the cigar-like joint he is smoking as a point of evidence, and says in mock seriousness, "There are two components to this spliff here, the rolling paper and the marijuana. What I want you to understand is that the rolling paper is by far the more expensive ingredient." Sometimes there are so many huge joints being passed around the dinner table that there are simply not enough lungs to smoke them all. The sight of them burning unused in the ashtrays would bring a cash-strapped high school kid in Minneapolis saving up for a ⅛ bag to tears.

With grass so cheap and responsibilities so few, smoking is not limited to evenings. I quickly become accustomed to people lighting up at breakfast or lunch before going to work. As with prostitution, attitudes varied, and, of course, there were extremes. Some only smoked on special occasions, but on the other hand, one finds people like Sansta (a nickname), a 35-year-old Swede who could barely remember his real name. For the four months he was in Cambodia, he spent every waking moment buying, shredding, rolling, and smoking ganja.

Cambodia is not the perfect smoker's paradise, though. The most frequent complaint is the sketchy quality of much of the grass. "It's hay," complains one local connoisseur. "The cultivation techniques are really primitive. They haven't yet learned to cure it properly, so it arrives in the market dry and harsh. But," he concedes, "you can find some amazing buds. Hey, at a dollar a pound, it's still excellent value." The best stuff is reserved for export, and is most easily available in the port cities of Kompong Som (Sihanoukville), and Koh Kong, bordering Thailand. Getting access to the export-quality stuff, however, is just a bit harder than strolling through the market; it requires contacts with the people who handle it, and who are willing to redirect part of an order for the domestic market. But this was beyond the motivation or ambition of the Majestic smokers, who contented themselves with large amounts of "hay."

My introduction to harder drugs comes early in my first research visit to Phnom Penh. Over a meal with Eric, he suddenly freezes in the middle of his diatribe about how atheists and homosexuals are scum, while Catholics are merely naive. "Shit, I didn't realize the time. Hold on, I'll be right back." I relax for while, eavesdropping on the conversations around me. He returns just ten minutes later, looking relieved and pleased with himself; "I'm glad I remembered when I did. I'm all out of smack for tonight and my dealer's almost always dry by eight. I would've been really fucked if I hadn't gotten any." As if stepping out for a pack of cigarettes, my dinner companion left the table for a few minutes, and returned $50 poorer and one gram of pure, high-quality heroin richer.

After dinner, we head upstairs to the guesthouse where Eric is glad to introduce me to the world of smack. I watch as he pours some of the magic powder on the mirror and then uses a razor to form it into two lines. Eric informs me that, "Heroin is much more potent if you inject it but it's also messier than snorting. It's so cheap here it's not worth getting into needles. We just snort it. This bag here is one gram, and the two lines on the mirror are about a twelfth of a gram each."

To me, 'a gram' always sounded like a tiny amount. But there is actually a sizable pile of powder in Eric's little bag. "I'm a casual user," he continues nonchalantly, "so this bag should last me about a month." Eric rolls up a red 500 *riel* note and uses it to snort one line into his nose. Hesitantly, I follow. The sensation is a bit ticklish, but not unpleasant, although it has a strange chemical taste. Eric vacuums up the scraps left on the mirror. "Waste not, want not," he laughs. "Your first time probably won't affect you very much, so you'll have to try again tomorrow."

Unsurprisingly, levels of heroin use vary. At two or three times a week, Eric is a moderate user. He is disciplined enough to keep himself within a very mild state of addiction. Most of the Majestic crowd uses smack only infrequently—perhaps a couple of times a month as an added high when going out, or a pick-me-up tonic before class. Heavy users, although atypical, are still in evidence. A teacher who is one of the many casual users of smack tells us that, "Philippe came by last night. I was shagging this pretty young thing from Tool Kok when he knocked on the door. He was in rough shape—he'd run out of smack and his dealer's out of town. It was something like eight hours since his last fix, and he didn't look good. I had about half a gram left. On the spot he mixed it with bottled water—tap water isn't sanitary, you know—and injected it into his hand. The little bird I was with couldn't believe it."

Steve, who only snorts heroin very occasionally, speaks with awe; "Philippe's quite a guy. He'll probably return double what he borrowed. He comes from some super-wealthy family in France. He's been on smack since 1985 and he's up to shooting half a gram four times a day."

Eric is outraged. "You mean enough smack for me to snort for two or three months, he takes in one day? Injects in one day?" The fact that Philippe is *injecting* two grams a day, rather than snorting, is a phenomenal amount. Reiner notes that, "He's saving a lot of money being a junkie in Cambodia rather than France." And Steve adds, "That's why he came here. He can do a lot with the money he saves by buying smack at Cambodian prices. And don't forget one thing—the two grams a day is just to avoid getting sick, not to actually get high."

One factor limiting heroin intake is that it impairs sexual function. At Champagne, I witness Eric's novel solution to this problem. He has joined a group at Champagne even though he is impotent from an earlier line of smack. A stunning Vietnamese girl he has taken home before saunters over and looks deeply into his dazed eyes. "I like this one," he says to me. "Nice tight pussy, cute little tits. I wouldn't mind taking her home tonight but I know I'd never get it up." Suddenly he has an inspiration and recruits me to translate. Although I have yet to learn the Vietnamese word for "impotent", I get the point across; Eric is unable to have sex, but he would like to pay the girl $5, instead of the usual $10–$15, just to sleep next to him.

She is suspicious, but I convince her of Eric's current physical limitation. I translate her response to Eric. "She's going to try and find someone for full payment. If nothing turns up, she'll go with you. But if you try anything after promising not to, she'll cut your dick off." Still high on the heroin and completely incapable of intercourse, Eric smiles in the knowledge that he and his organ are safe.

While people stick to fairly consistent schedules in their ganja and heroin intake, the use of prescription drugs from the pharmacies tends to be just for special occasions, experimentation, and, occasionally, sickness. Evelyn tells me of her first time using a depressant called Rohypnol; "I thought it might be fun to teach a lesson slightly mellowed. I tried to time it so that it would hit only toward the end of the class. There was about ten minutes left when it hit, and I could barely stand up. I started mumbling incoherently. Luckily, there was a Khmer teacher who co-taught with me. He stepped in and taught the rest of the lesson while I stood there and nodded and smiled." Steve tells me of giving an amphetamine called Ritilin to his girlfriend; "The stuff gets Lan horny as fuck. And if she has a toke on a spliff as well, she goes over the top; she has these multiple orgasms—it's wild."

As with the sexual excesses, it is less the specific stories that express people's attitudes, but rather the consistent, casual references to chemicals that sprinkle normal, everyday conversations. Picking just a few out of my notes;

"It's best to do a line of smack just after shagging."

"My student gave me a couple of kilos [of marijuana] from his uncle's field. It's shit gear though."

"I shouldn't have taken that speed before going to TK. My dick was all shriveled up and the girls were going crazy trying to get it hard and I was bouncing all over the cardboard walls."

113

"It's a good thing I had some smack left, or I never would've been able to stay awake for that second class."

"I was walking through the market, trying to think of what I could buy for my mates when I go back to Australia. When I passed by the ganja stall, my first thought was, 'Yeah, that'd be cool. I'll bring them a few ounces of smoke.' For that split second I totally forgot it's illegal in normal countries."

"I'm not addicted. I just take a little, you know, medicine, when I start to feel sick from not having my medicine for a couple of days."

Most of the people I met are able to handle their drug taking and still keep their jobs. But there are others who are simply unable to keep it together in the face of Phnom Penh's onslaught of drugs and sex. Mike is a likeable, under-educated English bloke. He is one of the few people I meet who, at 19, is young enough to have sex with women actually older than he is. While none of the people who hang out at the Majestic lead the lives of Trappist monks, I see a disturbing difference between their antics and Mike's frequent habit of getting dead drunk in a brothel and sleeping in the hot sweaty cubicle until early morning, when he drags himself back home. The morning of Christmas Eve, I notice Mike asleep on the wooden couch of the guesthouse balcony. A closer inspection reveals that he is passed out in the very picture of self-abusive decadence; his arm is draped over the side of the bench with his hand wallowing among seven or eight empty beer bottles. Eric's smack mirror and razor on the porch table are nice touches.

Downstairs in the restaurant, Eric is eating breakfast before going to work. I know that the white shirt is part of the school dress-code, but with his black tie, short blonde hair, and the strap of his school bag running diagonally across his chest, he looks disturbingly like some rotund fascist. When I tell him about Mike, this overweight, sexist bigot suddenly transforms into a loving Swiss grandmother. We both rush upstairs to the balcony where he says, with uncharacteristic sensitivity, "Oh my goodness, wake up Mike, you've over-slept!" He rushes to Mike's side to help him up. I don't pick up Mike's mumbled protest but Eric responds, "I know to-day's Christmas Eve, but you can't just give yourself the day off." Eric continues heroically trying to save his friend from himself but finally gives up and goes to class, leaving Mike comatose on the couch. I was touched by the concern this militaristic, racist, homophobic, child molesting smack addict showed toward his friend.

Seventh Heaven Lakeside Trip
April 6, 1997

With fewer reservations regarding drugs, I commit to 'researching' this topic more thoroughly than the brothels. My first step is the marijuana stalls at the market. I call a moto to take me to Russian Market, properly called Tool Tom Poong Market. We head south on Monivong from the guesthouse, soon crossing Sihanouk Boulevard—a major east-west artery. Moving on, the buildings tend to be lower and longer than those downtown. The stores are bigger, but less fashionable and more industrial. There are also a few very large, newer buildings—most of which are nightclubs or hotels—and even a couple of three or four-story factories and office buildings. Continuing south we turn right onto Mao Tse Tung Boulevard. This area is a bit more industrial than other parts of the city, and on both sides of the street we pass shop after shop de-voted to selling construction steel and cement. Nevertheless, the occasional newer, four-story building, or large restaurant or hotel, sprouts up among the older houses like flowers on a lawn.

At the immense and ornate Tool Tom Poong wat, we turn left onto a dirt road. A couple of bone-rattling, dusty minutes later, we arrive at the market. The interior is a huge area; stall after stall in long rows, with the products arranged in easily

Off the Rails in Phnom Penh

identifiable zones. Walking toward the market's center, I have already passed through the motorcycle spare parts section, the electronic goods section, the raw cloth section, and the hardware section. There is an amazing selection of products to buy for anyone with the money to spend, and/or the time and inclination to haggle. One stall catches my eye with a display of animal skins splayed out onto crossed twigs hanging from the front rafter. Looking down at the main counter, I see a variety of jars and packets containing various twigs, woods, barks, leaves, liquids, and a wide array of medicinal or flavor-enhancing herbs. My eyes rest on a packet containing something that looks a lot like marijuana. The proprietress, a bent and gnarly old woman with a bright face and a wide, half-toothless smile, informs me that it is indeed "gaan-cha" as the Khmers call it. Of course she invites me to buy it—all 90 grams or so, for two dollars. While I stumble over the grams-ounces conversion, recalling college days and scraping $50 together for an eighth of an ounce, she pulls down a large parcel from the shelf above her. This packet contains 1 kilogram of marijuana, and it can be mine—no bargaining necessary, for $20. Here it is, 2.2 pounds, over 35 ounces, of grass for $20. While no expert, I am sure that the US retail price of the packet I hold in my hands must be well over $2,000. Much as I like a bargain, I decline the kilo, but I do take a sniff of the smaller packet and see that it is indeed potent marijuana. After parting with two whole dollars, I am the proud owner of over three ounces of decent grass.

Following a trail well established by others before me, I take my stash to "the lake." Beng Kok (Lake Beng) is on the northern edge of the city. The Tool Kok brothels lie on its northern shore, while the eastern shore hosts an assortment of 'mellow' guesthouses. I get on the moto and we head off. We return to the Majestic area and then continue north, passing the 'highway' to the airport, and the city's landmark Calmette Hospital—alarmingly dilapidated, but apparently still functional. A short time later, we turn left onto a dirt road. It barely merits the compliment; if we were outside Phnom Penh, I would call it a wide jungle trail.

After a roller-coaster ride through the ruts and gullies, the moto drops me off at Seventh Heaven Restaurant and Guesthouse. I enter and walk through the hall onto the large restaurant patio. It is at this moment that I fully and almost physically feel how easy it would be to just drop out of life and stay here in Cambodia. The restaurant looks out onto the large, tranquil lake, and there are hammocks set up so you can just lie there and watch the day go by. Travelers and residents are sitting alone or in small groups, talking and smoking huge reefers. There is an almost reverential silence, as if it was some sort of temple to complete and utter passivity. The rooms are cheap, as is the food. With the price of grass so low, an individual with $250 to spare can comfortably spend a month on the lake doing nothing but smoking ganja all day. Looking around, I suspect that some of the people here have been doing just that.

Finding a table near the lake, I order my meal. The food is merely average, but the lake makes it a pleasant place to eat. I chat with some of my fellow diners, sharing my stash with them—although they have plenty of their own. This is an easy place to spend a few hours—or days, or months; a cool breeze from the lake, the open waters with quaint visions of Cambodian life on the far banks, cheap food, and an inexhaustible supply of marijuana. As the afternoon wears on and the sun heads down, it all starts to make perfect sense. Stoned and completely at ease, I realize the idiocy of a career in business journalism. The only sensible thing to do is to spend the rest of my life here on the lakeside smoking grass. As the dusk light fades, I manage to head back to the Majestic to start packing for my upcoming retirement by the lake.

I go up to my room and look out the window onto the less-than-picturesque neighborhood outside. As I wistfully long to be back at Seventh Heaven with a bong in my hands, I slowly come to realize the ease with which I could be sucked into a pleasant, but ultimately unfulfilling life here in Phnom Penh.

Merry Jane's Marijuana Pizza
April 10, 1997

Having successfully escaped Seventh Heaven, I am ready for one more crucial piece of 'field research.' Joe has agreed to take me to Merry Jane's and the two of us stroll in and sit down. On the surface, it is like a hundred thousand unpretentious pizza joints back home. Joe has been here before, and he once again pleads with me not to order my pizza "extra happy." He warns that I am underestimating "the power of the pizza." I am unswayed, and when the waitress comes, we order sodas and a large pizza—one half "mildly happy," and the other half "extra happy."

Joe and I chat while waiting for our order. He tells me of the first time he ordered "extra happy." "I went home not feeling anything special. I sat down at my desk to correct some homework. About two hours later, I suddenly found myself face down on the floor. I crawled—crawled! to my bed. I managed to get on the bed and just lay there watching the sounds come into the room. No bullshit, the traffic noises just kind of floated in and hovered near the ceiling. People talking, those sounds slithered in through the window and oozed onto the floor. The music from the ice cream seller, well that marched in the window and marched right out the door. It was all completely weird, but I could handle it. All hell broke loose when the gunshot flew in and landed right on the bed next to me. That freaked me out. So I crawled, or maybe I walked, I'm not sure, to the couch in the other room. That's where Sothea [his girlfriend at the time] found me.

"She's going on, 'Joe, no good! Joe go pizza no good. Joe dumb-dumb no good.' All I could do was lie there going, 'Uhhhhhh.' It wasn't exactly a lullaby, but her ear-bashing put me to sleep. I was on the couch until the next morning, and when I woke up she was still having a go at me like she'd been sitting there for six hours straight. You know, it's still not too late; we can pick off most of the 'extra happy' from your half."

Undaunted, I dive in as soon as our order arrives. The pizza, as pizza, is lackluster. As a vehicle for the wondrous herb, though, it serves its purpose well. Finely chopped pieces of choice ganja form a layer between the tomato sauce and the cheese. The tastes of stringy cheese, unremarkable tomato sauce, thin crust, and leaf after leaf of pungent ganja provide a unique, if not delicious, culinary experience.

The two of us are full and a quarter of the pizza remains uneaten. I want to continue on principle; it is shocking to waste so much ganja. After all, there are skate punks in Milwaukee dying for a toke. But Joe assures me that I've had enough—more than enough—and suggests we relax and let the meal digest. We order more sodas, and discuss Cambodian politics.

The conversation continues until the THC starts to take hold, and things start to get blurred around the edge. Joe and I then take the short ride along the riverside to the Stagecoach, one of the 'classy' riverside expat restaurants, where we will undergo the full force of our meal. Today is a perfect day to sit at one of the outdoor tables. The weather is warm but not hot, and the view of the waterfront is relaxing. Along the river we can see two or three small shrines with their graceful and exotic lines. It is soothing to just sit and contemplate the vast expanse of sky that marks this yet-undeveloped capital city.

Looking inside the restaurant, I notice a group of Frenchmen; Jean Marc—the guy we saw at the shooting range, two colleagues, and their boss. I know of them from my work in Saigon, and recall that they have an upcoming trade show here in Phnom Penh. They are chatting over drinks and I sit, happily dazed, watching them. There is something unusual, but strangely familiar, in the way they interact. The boss is cool and always in control of the conversation. Jean Marc laughs easily and follows his boss's leads shrewdly. The third is a large oafish-looking brute who appears lost, laughing at the boss's jokes only after Jean Marc has given him the cue. And the fourth is a weaselly-looking character who seems to be constantly searching for some kind of advantage.

Turning to look out over the river, I suddenly realize the great danger I'm in. Right here in the Stagecoach, I have unwittingly stumbled upon the core of the Corsican-French Mafia in Southeast Asia. Their boss is the godfather, Jean Marc his trusted lieutenant, the third guy the brainless muscle of the operation, and the fourth, the wily consigliere. The key question—the question that will decide whether I survive this night or not—is whether they are aware that I know. The ganja may have saved my life in that I am too numb to make any outward sign of fear or recognition. Then again, I curse myself and the ganja for leaving me so vulnerable in the face of this life-threatening situation. I play it cool, not alarming anyone, just going about my business normally. This is pretty easy because nothing more is expected of me other than sitting upright and maintaining my breathing.

The minutes drag on. I consider writing a last will and testament and passing it to Joe. But I don't know if I would be able to write in my state, nor would I be able to explain it away if the gangsters find it. So I just wait. After a decent interval, I tell Joe that I'm ready to leave. Even though I'm not confident in my ability to walk, I believe that leaving the area will be safer than staying where I might slip up and get myself in serious trouble with the Corsicans. As we get up, Joe notices my concern and asks if I'm all right. Then comes the most horrifying thought of all; What if Joe is one of them as well? I almost cry out in despair. Well, I think fatalistically, we all have to go sometime; I just hope it will be quick and painless. I'm resigned and relaxed now, already mourning the end of my short but interesting life, as Joe drives me to heaven knows where. I just close my eyes and wait for it to be over. When Joe stops in front of the guesthouse, I don't know whether to feel relief or anger. Does this mean that I really will survive? Or is this just some cruel trick before I am disposed of? Joe drops me off and I walk into the guesthouse as he parks his bike. Surely, they won't kill me here. I begin to feel safe. Quickly, but without panicking, I make my way to my room. Locking the door and moving the bed away from the windows, I get under the covers and pray that I will be delivered.

Work

Even in Phnom Penh's permissive atmosphere, sexual and chemical debauchery would be no fun if, as is the case in other parts of the world, they constantly led to problems at work. For many expats, part of the joy of Phnom Penh is that not only can they indulge in outrageous behavior, but they can also finance all of their activities locally.

For those who wander into Cambodia without a specific career goal, teaching English is the natural path to take. Although it is possible to come to Cambodia and find 'serious' work, few of the Majestic crowd have either the skills or ambition to look beyond standing in front of a classroom for a couple hours a day to make a living.

The English-teaching environment in Phnom Penh is as carefree as the chemical and sexual environments. While plenty of foreign teachers are competent and conscientious, a great number of the teachers I meet are either unqualified or uninterested, or both. With few exceptions, this is not much of a hindrance to their finding employment. Mike, for example, did not lose his job over his self-declared, heroin-and-alcohol-induced Christmas vacation. After three straight days of missed classes, he got "one last chance" from the school. Finally, when he skipped two more days without even calling, they let him go. As Joe puts it; "Teaching English in Cambodia doesn't have a lot of requirements, but showing up is

121

key." Mike was able to find work with another school quite easily. Although he dropped out of high school in England to earn money on a construction site, Mike was hired to teach a business course that borders on university Economics. On one occasion, a more dedicated teacher complained—foolishly— to the group at the table eating lunch before their afternoon classes about having had only five minutes to prepare for his upcoming class. "That's five minutes too many, mate," came Mike's response.

Within my first few hours in Phnom Penh I hear Rick, a veteran, speak with a new arrival. The new arrival asks, "You just arrive in Cambodia?"

"Nah, I've been here for two years. I just went home for a visit and now I have to look for work again. No problem, though. You can get work pretty fucking easy in Cambodia. I better get it quick though, 'cos after this coffee, I've got about five dollars left. But it's all right, I can run up a bill at the guest-house and eat cheap. Besides, this is Cambodia. It's the only country where you can show up with no job and nothing but a few bucks in your pocket and not feel like a total fucking loser. Hell, I could even go get laid for two bucks and still have enough until my first paycheck."

The new arrival then states his intention to learn Khmer. "You want to learn Khmer?" Rick is taken aback by the very idea of it. "Just get a piece of ass and have her teach you." Both were soon working at one of Phnom Penh's largest English schools.

A story from Evelyn about her first teaching job proves just how "pretty fucking easy" it is to get work; "I'd just arrived here and I'd been out drinking with the guys the night before. So I'm on the porch feeling like shit with this evil hangover. I roll a joint and start toking heavily to counteract the nuclear explosions going on in my head. In the middle of my second joint, I look up to see this well-dressed Khmer guy examining me. My first thought was, 'Oh God, I'm in trouble with the police for smoking pot.' But then I remembered where I was and I dismissed that for the totally ridiculous notion it was.

"Anyway, he smiles and introduces himself as Mr. Lam, and I'm feeling a bit embarrassed because I'm wearing nothing but a *kromah* around my waist and a ragged T-shirt with no bra. He sits down and says he's from Prince Monivong Language School, and he's looking for teachers and do I know anyone who may be interested. When I tell him I'm looking for work myself, he goes, 'Great, when are you available?' I tell him any time's fine and he says, 'Wonderful, can you come on Wednesday at five-thirty?' 'To interview?' 'No, to teach. We pay six dollars an hour.' I couldn't believe it. Apparently, white skin and the ability to string together a few words in basic English are the only criteria, and I've just got a job. So then I'm trying to act professional even though I'm wearing nothing but dirty old rags and there's ganja smoke everywhere from the huge spliff in the ashtray. 'OK he says, I'll be watching your first class because we have very high standards at Monivong School, and I must keep the quality.' It was hilarious. I was so fucked up and this guy comes in and gives me a job."

The lack of quality teachers and the heavy demand for foreigners (of any nationality) to teach English means that even schools which actually screen for qualifications end up with some real losers. For example, at the New Zealand International Center for Education (NICE), an aid-funded school which pays high wages, it is an open secret that many, if not most, of the teacher certifications that are presented are fakes. One applicant went so far as to submit a forged MBA. "It's a stretch when they have me teach medical statistics," he says laughing, "but the fucking Khmers don't know the difference." A longtime teacher at NICE tells me of another applicant who submitted a photocopy of a diploma with his name appearing at a visible angle, thus marking it as an obvious fake. "If he hadn't tried to give himself a masters in linguistics, they probably would have let him get away with it."

It is a real pleasure to meet a teacher at NICE named Dirk. A naturalized Kiwi with a heavy accent from his native Spain, Dirk is an engaging and popular teacher. His certification, he declares proudly, is, "a very good forgery." With perverse pride typical to the Majestic crowd, he cheerfully describes being fired from his previous job. "I'd just gotten a huge paycheck, so I brought three sexy young girls home from TK. We were up all night shagging. In the morning I [sic] was almost time to teach my early class, so I sent the girls home, took a line of smack, and went in [sic] school. I forgot to shower, so I must have looked so bad. No lesson plan of course, so I just started conversation on the first topic that came into my head. I guess I must have taken too much smack. When the school administrator walked in and saw 'LET ME BE YOUR DOG' and 'RAPE MY ANUS WITH YOUR THUMB' on the whiteboard, well, it was pretty much over for me at that school."

Over meals at the Majestic, I meet plenty of other English teachers who need a few English lessons themselves. One German has an accent so heavy I can barely understand him. I also meet a Romanian who tells me that, "I been teach English in Cambodia since four years."

Flotsam

> "God, I'm gonna miss this place. After all, in Switzerland I'm just some short, fat, unemployed nob. But here, . . ."

The foreigners who choose to live in a warped and dysfunctional environment like Phnom Penh might also be expected to exhibit these characteristics personally. Broadly speaking, expatriates in Phnom Penh fit into one of two categories. The first consists of professionals sent to Cambodia by their employers (either government agencies, NGOs, or private companies) or entrepreneurs who come to Cambodia with the capital and skills to get a business started. The second category consists of people who just drift into Cambodia and stay, or others attracted—like flies to shit—by all the stories of cheap girls or cheap drugs. During my trips to Cambodia I ignored the professionals and focused on the detritus.

Within this second group, I made an additional distinction between 'adventurers' and 'lifers.' Adventurers are in Cambodia temporarily, even if they stay for a long time. They get a kick out of the music or the politics, or the girls or the drugs—or any combination of, or all of the above. But they are cognizant of the outside world, and expect to return to it eventually. Also, importantly, they have the skills to survive outside of Cambodia. Lifers, on the other hand, do not. They are here to stay—many of them because they do not have the ambition or the ability to handle life anywhere else.

125

Off the Rails in Phnom Penh

Steve is the quintessential adventurer. He is an Australian, solidly built around a smallish frame. On first meeting him, I am most impressed by the energy he exudes, even though he is already finishing the second of what were obviously, from the generous roaches left, huge joints. He is divorced, and has a two-year-old daughter whom he misses terribly. Steve was employed as a senior accountant in a respected Australian firm for eight years. But his sense of living is simply too large to be accommodated by a nine-to-five office job. Taking advantage of the freedom of his divorce and some money saved up, he left Australia to seek adventure in the world beyond Adelaide. Cambodia is his first stop of any appreciable length of time, and he is enjoying it immensely. Even though he left the corporate world to shag prostitutes, toke pot, and snort smack in Cambodia, Steve is a professional when it comes to work, and is highly regarded at the schools where he teaches. I am consistently inspired by Steve's zest for living, even if I occasionally question the avenues by which he expresses that passion. He thinks nothing of dancing all night with Lan—the 16-year-old brothel girl who reciprocates his deep love for her—then teaching a couple of morning classes, then going to Tool Kok for sex with two, maybe three girls, finally returning home late afternoon to chat and make love with Lan—who has spent the day sleeping off the previous night's excesses. Steve could make it anywhere in the world, but he loves Cambodia because it is one place which definitely accommodates his passion for adventure.

Eric too is an adventurer. One night over dinner, I chat with him as he fondles the girls he has brought back from a Tool Kok brothel. He tells me that, despite his desire to stay, he feels it is time to go back to Switzerland and get an MBA. "That way, when I graduate I can get a real job with a company here. Fuck this English teaching bullshit. And it means I'll be close to this." With that, he runs his finger down one girl's left breast, covered only by a tight polyester blouse. "God, I'm gonna miss this place. After all, in Switzerland I'm just some short, fat, unemployed nob. But here . . ."

It is the lifers that represent the true spirit of expatriates in Cambodia. In a conversation with Joe and Jeff, I mention that there are also lifers in Viet Nam. "But it's different. They're just guys who've found a good ride and they're enjoying it. This guy named Clark is a perfect example. He used to be a real estate agent in the US. A couple of years ago he left for Viet Nam to teach English, and he's been there ever since. He's got a low-stress job, makes good money, has his nice apartment, and a girlfriend who's out of his house by eleven every night in case the police come checking. It's like he's in semi-retirement. When you talk with him, he's coherent, he's healthy—he goes swimming three times a week, he's not that different from who he was in the States."

Jeff joins in; "But the guys here, they look fucking spent out, man. They've burned out so many brain cells and fucked so many fourteen-year-olds, they'll never be able to go back to the West. I mean, I love it here, but you look at the wrinkles and the eyes of these older guys here for good, and you just see that this place isn't healthy long term."

Joe tells us that, "Cambodia is the kind of place where the years just slip by. I mean, you've spent the last thirty years stoned, teaching English three hours a day. You wake up one morning and say, 'Jesus Christ, I'm sixty-five. What the fuck am I still doing here? Get this young girl out of my bed, I gotta go home.' I worry that Mike is headed for that. I can imagine thirty years from now, and Mike is still in deep shit with his visa. 'Mike, did you take care of your visa yet?' 'Nah, not yet.' 'How long are you over?' 'Well, I came in 1995, so it's about, oh, I don't know, thirty-two years.' 'Wow, so at a fine of three bucks a day, it's about a grand a year . . . just about thirty-two thousand dollars.' 'Yeah, well I managed to save up a few hundred before I got fired from my last job teaching English, but I just bought a motorbike, so I'm down to zero again. I'll figure something out. By the way, do you have five bucks I can borrow? Right, cheers mate.'

"You see these old guys teaching English for seven dollars an hour. Every month they spend about three hundred for their room and food, and a couple of hundred for the teenage whores they've bought out of the brothel. That still leaves plenty of pocket money for ganja and videos. That's how the guy in the downstairs apartment lives. He just sits in front of the video rolling spliffs with his eighteen-year-old girlfriend."

"Yeah," Jeff adds, "she spent about four years in the brothel before he bought her out. Where else is some fifty-year-old asshole going to live like that? Back in England? No way, that guy's here to stay."

To my inquiry about Mike's visa, Joe explains that, "Last year, he came into Cambodia from the Thai border at Koh Kong. It's not difficult, but it *is* illegal. You can't get an exit stamp from Thailand or an entry stamp from Cambodia—and you won't get a visa like at the airport. So, ever since he set foot in Cambodia, he's been an illegal immigrant. It's gonna be a nightmare for him to leave without taking care of it."

Jeff continues, "In the first month he was here, someone offered to take care of it for him for sixty bucks, but he figured that was too expensive, or he didn't have the cash, or whatever. Now, nine months later, he still has no visa—and at three bucks a day, he's looking at about eight hundred in fines and counting."

"Yeah, and he's got about zilch saved up to cover it," adds Joe. "I like the guy, but what a fucking idiot, man!"

Mike, despite his irreparable hopelessness, is a likable guy, and I pray that he will not end up like Dick—a 47-year-old American-born New Zealander, who is also one of the most pathetic human beings I have ever had the displeasure to meet. Dick's utter lack of charm leaves him friendless, and his complete incompetence often leaves him jobless—even in the Phnom Penh education racket. It is pitiful as he explains his plans to set up this or that business, while he cannot even save the money to replace his worn out briefcase. We all joke about his habit of reading newspapers in hotel lobbies so he can pretend to be an important businessman without actually spending any money.

But at least Dick earns enough to buy the companionship of a young girl for an afternoon, although even the most hardened professionals cannot hide their dislike for him. Evelyn explains it this way; "He despises the girls for making him pay because he understands very clearly that they wouldn't even look at him otherwise. I don't think he's ever had a consensual lover. These five dollar fucks are the closest he'll ever come to a relationship. So who does he take out his frustrations on? The poor girls who haven't learned to avoid him yet."

In complete contrast to Henrik's misplaced romanticism, Dick represents a textbook case of the ugliest version of the brothel patron; a bitter man who uses young girls' rented bodies out of fear, spite, or anger against all those women who—unlike the brothel girls—are free to refuse him.

Another teacher who knew him in Thailand said that he developed a reputation among the Bangkok schools as an incompetent instructor and, among the bar girls there, as a cheap and unpleasant customer. So, he moved to Cambodia. Later, while living in Thailand, friends and I would see guys in girlie bars desperately trying to pick up hookers, but too cheap to buy them and too pathetic to charm them. I would tell friends I was with, "That guy has Cambodia written all over him." Joe sums it up; "Cambodia is a great place for losers like Dick to come and act like they matter. For five dollars, they can strut around with beautiful women, and if they're conscious, they can get a job teaching English. It's a haven for these guys who wouldn't last a second in any other country."

Losers or not, Cambodia does seem to attract a disproportionate share of humanity's leftovers. Reiner is technically brilliant, an excellent salesman, and unshakably principled. But he has a lot to work on in the relationship management department. By my last trip to Cambodia, Reiner and Richard, one of his business partners, have had a falling out. The cause of the problem was Reiner's undiplomatic handling of a certain delicate situation in their computer software company. Richard, the aggrieved partner, shows us some interesting material and explains; "So, here's the deal. We wired three thousand dollars to a company in the US for some software development. Well, they kept screwing up, so Reiner wanted to get the money back. They agreed but said we had to wait 'til the end of the monthly billing cycle. But that wasn't fast enough for Reiner so he starts sending them faxes. Here, look. The first one's bad enough but they get worse as they go along."

Steve and I look over the e-mails and faxes, which range from amusing and unusual to obscene and absurd. Even before the relationship deteriorated, Reiner's messages were unconventional, to say the least;

> *I'm drunk as I write this, but don't worry, I'm in full control of my faculties. I had a meeting with Ms. Wang Chi Li of Caltex Cambodia, and I think that they may come on as a client. She's a beautiful 25-year-old Malaysian Chinese, and I want you to give her extra good service. I expect to have my way with her by the end of the first month of the contract.*

After things start going wrong, Reiner's e-mails become abusive;

> *. . . now I realize that you are just some fly-by-night promise much, deliver little CoRpOrAtIoN. So you are the one incorporated as WorldSoft. The desk next to you. Who sits there? What name have you given that dodgy enterprise? And the boss of all this, is he prepared to go to jail on fraud charges? I want you to call me, or better yet, have Mr. X call me, so we can straighten out this situation.*

As the relationship deteriorated further, the communications become even more aggressive;

> *You are my most stupid mistake. I must take the blame for trusting someone like you . . . You know what they say, once a monkey, always a monkey . . . If the money is not in my account by April 5, get ready for some real crisis management.*

They get more and more threatening;

Open your eyes and listen very carefully. You now have very little time to bail out. You may pray to God that I will be satisfied with you returning the money and set aside my burning desire to inflict further punishment on you. If I do, you better watch out, because you know that I will come for you real hard.

"If I got this in the mail, it'd go straight into the trash," Steve says to Richard. "Of course you didn't get your money back." We flip through more of the faxes;

You know what? You may now file for special protection from the FBI. Also, you may be obligated to notify your insurance company of the additional risks. Otherwise your policy may be invalid. One hour from Phnom Penh to Bangkok, eight hours to San Francisco, one hour to Santa Rosa. I can't wait.

Remember to lock the door behind you, stay away from windows, and don't talk to strangers. And in particular remind Sean in marketing to hide. I want his skin real bad.

And in the end, they become too ridiculous to take seriously, even as threats;

Are you going to enjoy explaining to the FBI why someone came all the way from Cambodia to fistfuck your shitheads? . . . Remember Aliens 2? "It will not help."

While the specifics of Reiner's behavior were unique in Phnom Penh, his general maladjustment was not. I often wondered whether Cambodia destabilized otherwise rational people, or whether dysfunctional characters were naturally drawn here as if to a magnet. Whichever the case, any idiosyncrasies a person brings into the country have free rein to fully develop in Phnom Penh's unbalanced atmosphere. I also had to wonder about my own fascination with the country, and the effect it was having on me and others around me. A definitive list of all the characters I met in Phnom Penh and all of their antics could produce a book in itself. This eminently entertaining cast is a fiction writer's dream. The problem is that most of them are too unbelievable to use in a book. Just a sample of this crew includes;

Bill, a New York cab driver who always takes his annual vacation in Cambodia. Bill has the ability to talk *literally for hours* in a gruff, barely coherent monotone about nothing of interest to anyone.

Sansta, the pot-smoking Swede. He decided to apply for work teaching English, and I helped him with his resume. This 35-year-old listed a lifetime total of 13 months of work experience.

Giovanni, an Italian soldier left over from UNTAC. He had such a bad reputation for drunken brawls and other bad behavior that one of the English language newspapers announced his departure from the country.

Samuel, a nervous and secretive South African and his son, Richard. As far as we can tell, Samuel has kidnapped his son from his estranged wife and the two are hiding out in Cambodia.

Harry, a man known to most of the expats only as "Child Molester." He spends hours at the Majestic bragging about finding the youngest girls in the brothels, and describes making them cry with all the hideous things he does to them before, during, and after intercourse. Even in Cambodia, he is considered bad news.

Helmut, a German 'Buddhist' who each week has trouble deciding whether to spend his Sunday meditating in the monastery or fornicating in Tool Kok. "If I ever get AIDS, I'll just stop smoking and enter the monastery to meditate. You know, these things are really just in your head."

Rod, an American who has not left Southeast Asia since the Viet Nam War. He talks of his days as a mechanic in the Marines as if they were of any interest to the assembled English teachers. One of his hobbies is eating live geckos, the small lizards that are ubiquitous in Southeast Asia. "In the Marines, we learned to swallow anything."

Suffice it to say that Cambodia is a wonderful place to meet many 'interesting' people. I found, though, that after a while this constant stream of human wreckage actually became tedious.

Khmers

> "Pholla said, '. . . I'd better defend myself.' For the next two weeks, she walked around the room wearing her bra on the outside of her sarong as some kind of curse protection."

It is not only the evil antics of politicians and the depraved misadventures of foreigners that produce a surreal atmosphere in Phnom Penh. Ordinary Khmers themselves do an excellent job of contributing to the environment which I found so bizarre. Interactions with—and conversations about—the Khmers helped flesh out some aspects of these people we found so gentle yet so impossible to understand. Not only to an interloper like myself, but even to many long-term residents, Khmers remain largely a mystery. In the words of Avi, a Khmer speaker and one of the more thoughtful English teachers I met; "After all the time I've spent here, all the time I've spent studying with Khmer teachers, working with Khmers, chatting with *moto* drivers, prostitutes, mechanics, the people at RAC, and businesspeople, whatever—I still have pretty much no clue what these people are about."

Pamela, a businesswoman from America who is fluent in Khmer (and who has never been to the Majestic in her life) offers some insight as to why this is so; "The Khmers have an uncanny ability to completely ignore something that makes them uncomfortable. So if as a foreigner you make them feel shy or nervous, then you simply don't exist. And if you ask difficult questions about Khmer culture or society, then these questions also don't exist. But that shyness isn't the whole explanation. Even with people who feel comfortable around me, even with people who are trying very hard to be open, it still feels like we're not connecting. It's like we're talking a different language; I don't mean Khmer or English, but the whole structure of thinking is different. Basically I really enjoy working and talking with Khmers, but I always come away with the feeling that I missed something."

Ronald, an Australian businessman with extensive experience working in Asia makes another comment about Khmer-foreign interactions; "They are kept to a minimum. Everywhere else that I've worked, I've been able to meet people and make friends—well, acquaintances at first—very easily. You know, people want to speak to a foreigner for all sorts of reasons—whether it's to practice their English, or because they think they can profit financially from the relationship, or they're genuinely curious about who we are and what we think, or they want to be a good representative of their country, or they just want a chance to talk to this exotic being from somewhere far away. Everywhere else I've been overwhelmed by students and colleagues—or just people on the street—striking up conversations and inviting me for drinks and dinners. That's great, but it can also be frustrating because sometimes you just want to be left alone. When I started work in Cambodia, I was actually a bit disappointed, because they really do leave you alone. Part of it's this shyness, it's almost like fear. But it also seems they're just not that interested in foreigners. Or if they are, they don't show it. Or perhaps things are so different for us, they don't even know how to frame the question. I just don't know."

Serge Thion's book *Watching Cambodia* provides the best advice about trying to make sense of Cambodia; "The country is like a labyrinth . . . But there is no final word, no hidden truth at the end. That would require entering all the gates of the labyrinth at the same time." So although I never found anyone who could guide me through the labyrinth, I was able to explore some of the maze myself. If I were to sum up all my impressions of Khmers into one sentence, I would say that they simply do not inhabit this physical plane of existence in the way other people do.

Put another way, the Khmer world consists of a broader reality than the one Europeans, North Americans, as well as their neighbors the Vietnamese and Chinese, are used to. Westerners especially tend to look at things in terms of simple, direct, physical cause and effect. Khmers see a much more complicated scenario. The Khmer world incorporates a supernatural side that Westerners are completely unable to fathom. A common term used to describe this phenomenon is "superstition." Joe, who has been with his girlfriend, Pholla, for a over a year, tells us how, "One night, we went to Champagne; after hearing all about Sothea [Joe's ex-girlfriend] from my landlady, she finally meets her. A week later, Pholla tells me she's been feeling under the weather for the past few days. 'Sothea must be putting curses on me.' But even worse was the time when a Champagne girl I'd brought home long before showed up at the house asking for a 'loan' of a few dollars. With Pholla in the room, I told her I couldn't do it because I loved my girlfriend and didn't want to make her angry. As soon as the Champagne girl left, Pholla said, 'Why did you do that. Now she'll hate me. I'd better defend myself.' For the next two weeks, she walked around the room wearing her bra on the outside of her sarong as some kind of curse protection. It looked absolutely ridiculous."

Tattoos are a common defensive maneuver among male Khmers. Throughout Cambodia it is common to see men with elaborate tattoos on their arms, chest, or back. The tattoos are monochromatic and made up of intricate patterns, diagrams, and text. They are quite beautiful. Evelyn tells us of the shock of discovering a series of marks tattooed into her Khmer boyfriend's hairline. Pou, her boyfriend who is an ex-solider, explains with Avi translating; "The purpose is to protect us when we go into battle. If you have a good set of tattoos, the bullets fly right past." Like all good articles of faith, this belief withstands evidence to the contrary; "One time a friend of mine was wounded. It was a good thing he had the tattoos. Imagine how much worse it would've been. He probably would've died."

Foreigners mock these superstitious beliefs at their own peril. The first time I meet Josh, Steve and I are sitting in the Majestic when a force of nature suddenly whirls itself into our presence. Steve addresses it as Josh, and then it begins spewing words frantically. If it were not Cambodia, I would consider Josh a lunatic.

"Fuck it, Steve, she's gone and I don't know where. And she's ready to have the baby any day—she could've dropped it already for all I know. So I don't even know if the kid's alive or dead, or where it is, or where she is, or anything. And it's like, good riddance you bitch. It was the stupidest argument, man, and now everything's completely fucked up and I might never even see the kid. I was taking the piss with Dirk about that string of beads she wears around her waist, you know, to ward off evil spirits and shit like that. We were making fun of how she has trouble putting it on with her stomach so big with the baby. So she gets all offended and fucks off. OK, so I'll let her stew at home for a while and then when she's calmed down I'll apologize, whatever. But I get home and she's gone. And you know what else is gone, the seven hundred dollars I saved for her and the baby. Stupid slag steals her own money and now she's gone."

This man has an amazing ability to speak at high intensity for an extended period without taking a breath; "Her sister just told me she ran off to her cousin's house. Yeah, fucking great. He's former KR, and the next day he nicked the cash and fucked off to Bantea Meanchey [a remote province largely controlled by the Khmer Rouge]. Now the money's gone, and I can't go back to England like I wanted to 'cos the stupid bitch won't have any money to feed the baby—and then the kid'll die 'cos the cunt is so fucking stupid. Can you believe it? 'Cos of a fucking good luck charm, she loses the money and now she has nothing. Well that's it. I'm gonna bring every taxi-girl I can find back to the house while she's gone. I'm gonna introduce the whores to the fucking neighbors. If she ever comes back, she'll be a fucking laughingstock. Now I have to start

.g those little shits again to get back the money she
from herself. Steve, I'm so sick of teaching, man. I'm so
.rned out. All I wanted to do was go back home and send
money until she came over. So now it's back to the fucking
classroom, staring into those faces and I know they don't understand a word and I just want to fucking slap them. It's a
good thing she wears that good luck charm."

Josh exits as rapidly as he entered and Steve turns to me
and says, "I've never seen him so pissed off, but don't worry
about it, they've been together two years, they've had grief
before. But he loves her. She'll be back and the kid'll be fine.
The thing is, she's Khmer and he still hasn't worked them out.
But that's not surprising."

Another aspect of the Khmer worldview which is as chal-
lenging to Westerners as their superstition, is their full and
living faith in reincarnation. Avi comes back from class one
day wearing a wide grin. "We were talking about religion. I
told them I'm Jewish, and explained that we don't eat pork or
shellfish. One student told me, very friendly like and helpful,
it's a pity I was born Jewish, because all that non-kosher stuff
is so delicious. Then he said, 'I hope in your next life you're
born something else so you can try pork and crab.' Isn't that
nice?"

Steve continues the theme; "A student of mine told the
class about how her sister was forced into marriage with some
guy during the Khmer Rouge time. They had one kid but she
hated him so they divorced right after the Vietnamese invaded.
So, now that she's divorced no other Khmer guy is even gonna
look at her. I still remember what my student said; 'She's lost
hope she'll be happy in this life. She's just waiting for it to
end so she can start again in the next one.'"

"That's part of the problem with Khmer politics," Joe states.
"Whatever happens, they can justify it with *karma* and reincarnation. I mean, some government official sells off a huge
chunk of forest. Either he was very good in his past life, and
the bribe from the lumber company's his reward in this life,
or he's evil, and he'll be reborn a slug in his next life. They
just don't have the incentive to see justice right here, right

now. I mean, if *karma* and Buddha will take care of it, why should I risk my life now? If Hun Sen is being a bastard, Buddha will punish him for it. We don't need to."

My layman's analysis makes a connection between this emphasis on spiritual existence and future (hopefully better) lives on one side, and the Khmers' seemingly high tolerance for physical privation on the other. The majority of Khmers appear to be relatively unambitious regarding material possessions. A stable supply of rice and a secure home seem to be about the pinnacle of material desire for much of Khmer society. Ambitious Khmers are more likely to seek power and prestige, rather than mere physical belongings. It is Cambodia's ethnic Chinese who are concerned with amassing something as trivial as wealth. Today, as it has been for centuries, Phnom Penh's commercial sector is dominated by Sino-Khmers.

The lackadaisical attitude of the Khmers toward material possessions stands in marked contrast to the attitude prevalent in Cambodia's neighbor and long-time rival, Viet Nam. With so many regulars at the Majestic having lived or traveled in Viet Nam, comparisons between the two countries are a common theme. Joe contends that, unlike the Khmers, the Vietnamese are easy to understand; "They are greedy. Blind, overwhelming greed is very simple to understand. Despicable, but simple." Trading stories about the Vietnamese passion for extracting money from foreigners is a favorite pastime at the Majestic;

"I was with a *Viet Khieu* [an overseas Vietnamese] friend in Hanoi during *Tet* [Vietnamese New Year] in '93. My friend translated what the loudspeakers were broadcasting; 'Comrades, during this *Tet* holiday, do not overcharge your fellow citizens [as is the usual practice]. Instead, gouge the foreigners.'"

"I was in a hotel in Dalat and this girl came down the hall selling candy. She really wanted to come into the room, so I thought, OK, whatever. About thirty seconds later, a cop showed up and snapped a picture. Then he said I had to pay a fine for having a prostitute in my room. I couldn't believe it, but I had no choice—the hotel had my passport. Fifty fucking dollars."

"People doing business in Viet Nam have this joke; What's the difference between Viet Nam and a casino? In a casino, you at least have a chance of not losing your money."

"I watched a vendor selling coconuts from his cart. Not knowing I spoke Vietnamese, he told this woman, 'Look at this foreigner watching us. Pay me five thousand (instead of the usual two) so he thinks that's the price. As soon as he pays, I'll give you the three thousand back.' I couldn't resist it. I didn't even want a coconut but I went up to buy one anyway and so he says, in English, five thousand. I told him, in Vietnamese, I knew what he'd said to the woman before and he was really pissed off. The fucker still wanted me to pay five thousand."

"Yeah, Viet Nam's incredible. From the instant you get off the airplane until the moment you leave, every single person tries to steal, extort, seduce, or lie their way into your pocket."

"Sure, you sometimes get overcharged here or in Thailand. But it's different from Viet Nam. Here it's a possibility. There it's a given."

I challenge Joe's view of those he tongue-in-cheek calls "my Vietnamese brothers" with the story of losing my wallet and having it returned to me with every *dong* inside. Joe responds, "Sure, there are some honest people in Viet Nam. About nine of them. The worst thing is that honest Vietnamese people don't have a chance. After you get to know the country, you just assume that everyone you meet is trying to rip you off."

In contrast, we all appreciate the absence of this atavistic greedy streak in our hosts, the Khmers. While this makes Cambodia a more comfortable environment than Viet Nam, there is a downside. Given their desire to improve their lot by any means necessary, the Vietnamese are often labeled "industrious." What I termed the Khmers' "tolerance for physical privation," others have tagged simply as laziness. Over a drink at an upscale expat bar, Pamela, the businesswoman with a long tenure in Cambodia—and a deep affection for the country—complains about her Khmer colleagues' lack of motivation. In a flash of utter exasperation she remarks bitterly that, "The only person who ever got the Khmers to work hard was Pol Pot, and look what he had to do." Beyond the shocking bad taste of that statement, there is an element of truth in this complaint of idleness—but it is a clear oversimplification. One can find examples of Khmers willing to forgo material gain not because of laziness, but because they place a higher value on non-material considerations.

As expected, this subject was explored most thoroughly at the Majestic in the context of sex. "If she can smell an extra dollar in it, a Vietnamese girl will go down on you like she's starving for it," says an extremely well-qualified commentator. "But Khmers just don't consider it, I dunno, proper, so they don't even consider charging extra for it. I still remember the first time I asked a Khmer girl to go down on me. She made this face, and said, 'What do I look like, some Vietnamese whore?'"

Even outside the world of sex, examples of this material/spiritual split are evident. A perfect case in point is this incident between Reiner and his ex-employee, Sopea—who worked as his combination Khmer teacher/'gopher' (as Dara does now). I find Reiner and Sopea in the Majestic one day having a heated discussion; Sopea says angrily, "I tell you before it no work, so why you tell me do it."

"Wait, wait," Reiner responds testily, "you said it was impossible, so I showed you how. I didn't say it was easy, but look," Reiner waves the small piece of chain-mail he's made, "it's possible to do."

In this typically hare-brained business scheme, Reiner is trying to manufacture chain-mail in Cambodia and then sell it in Europe and North America. Chain-mail is basically a cloth 'woven' out of thousands of small rings of metal, and Reiner hopes to sell this stuff to mediaeval wargames enthusiasts (jousting matches and fairs etc.), and sado-masochists and fetishists. The process of making chain-mail is labor intensive and Reiner wants Sopea to produce prototype models to get the business rolling. Cambodian labor, as personified by Sopea, may be cheap, but in this case not very productive. Sopea is unhappy with this assignment and looks with contempt at the collection of tiny metal rings before him. "No, cannot, it no possible. Cannot, cannot," he says firmly.

Reiner seems to come to a realization. "So it's possible to do, but not possible for *you* to do." He takes Sopea's grunt for a yes. "So maybe you can do it, but you don't want to."

Sopea, quieter now but still glaring, says, "My job teach you Khmer, not make shirt."

"OK, OK. Why don't you go for lunch now and I'll see you in the afternoon."

Sopea, mollified but still unhappy, tramps out of the restaurant. Reiner, in exasperation, takes a deep breath, leans back in the chair, and then explains the outburst. "See that, it's all part of this Khmer thing with power and advantage. Give them one iota of power over others, and they'll abuse it in seconds. This is just one side of it. He speaks English so, of course, he's an intellectual—part of the elite—which is above the peasants. So, it's totally unacceptable that I'd ask him to do anything like manual labor, like some illiterate. I mean, he'll sit for hours making those vocab flash cards without moaning, but ask him to do one fucking thing using his hands, and no way, he's too good for that. He's an intellectual. No wonder Pol Pot killed off everyone with an education. You know, I started this in Viet Nam before I left. My guy there thought it was stupid, but I was paying him, so he did it. No problem."

Reiner ended up firing Sopea and taking on Dara—a non-English speaker—who was therefore willing to perform a wider variety of tasks. But Reiner encountered problems of a different nature. He would occasionally ask Dara go to the local markets and sample the prices of various goods. One day, Dara politely tells Reiner that if he is sent to the markets in the morning, he will have to quit the job, no matter how much he needs the money. Reiner explains afterwards; "I can't send him in the morning because he might be the first person of the day to enter the shop. If he's the first one and he doesn't buy anything, then the shopkeeper will have bad luck all day. And he'll blame Dara, and curse him to have a lousy day as well." It was not laziness that prompted Dara to threaten to quit, but on the surface it could have been interpreted as such.

In another vein, this charge of laziness falls apart given the incredible energy Khmers bring to certain aspects of life. If the primary goal of a Khmer man is power, then the primary goal of a Khmer woman is to find a man to provide for her. And she will react passionately if that goal is threatened. As an example of the insane jealousy that apparently grips all Khmer women involved in non-prostitution relationships, Joe comes into the restaurant one night looking distraught. "This is the last straw," he says in exasperation. "Pholla's furious because she's finally got 'proof' I'm cheating on her. I told her I ate dinner at a guesthouse restaurant today and she instinctively associates guesthouses with places that men bring taxi-girls, so she's suspicious right away.

"When she asked me about the guesthouse, I told her it was near Olympic Market. She exploded. 'I know about that. You had that girl from Champagne. She lives near Olympic Market. You went and did her in the guesthouse. How could you do this to me?' And she starts bawling. I didn't know what she was talking about. So then she describes—in more detail than *I* could remember—some girl I'd brought back from Champagne a couple of times. Thinking about it, I vaguely remembered she mentioned living near the market. The landlady must've told Pholla everything about my past sex life. Eating dinner in a guesthouse near Olympic Market is Pholla's proof I'm out shagging other girls. It was too stupid to even argue about, so I just left the house. I suppose that only confirms my guilt."

Some of the other guys trade stories about this furious jealousy;

"I was just sitting there stoned, staring into space. Out of nowhere, Ratana accuses me of missing one of the girls I'd brought home before. 'Who you tink about? You leave me for her. Why you hurt me?'"

"I told Sothea I didn't like the pork she bought. I wasn't having a go at her or anything, I just said it was stringy. She gets angry and says so now I'll probably bring Malai back 'cos she always bought good pork. Unreal."

"A birthday card from an old friend of mine back home winds up torn up in the trash. She starts going on about how I've got a wife in America [completely untrue], and I'm so mean for putting love letters on my desk like that."

"This guy, one of my students, takes me out to dinner, and I have to convince Kanna that I'm not going to shag his sister."

Given the disastrous consequences of being abandoned, and the disturbing frequency with which it occurs, it is not surprising that this passion is expressed fiercely. Jeff tells me about one woman who used to be Pierre's girlfriend; "They were pretty steady for a while and really seemed to be in love. Then Pierre dumped her. She took it pretty well, even when she found out he started going out with a good friend of hers. She took it so well, that one night she even went over to his place for a shag. Afterwards, when he was asleep, she stabbed him in the leg with a knife. The hospital said it missed his artery by a couple of centimeters. If she'd cut it, he almost definitely would've bled to death." Again, we get the comparison with the Vietnamese. "A Vietnamese girl will steal all your money, but at least she won't kill you."

Even more disturbing than Pierre's encounter is the story Eric tells me about Andre and "Baby-Killer." "Andre had this girlfriend from Champagne, I don't remember her real name. She'd been seeing this Indian guy but supposedly dumped him for Andre. Anyway, she got pregnant and Andre was all excited—until a little Indian kid popped out. Andre dumped her and the Indian guy was long gone. So she's alone and broke, in pretty bad shape really. A couple of weeks later, the baby, um, kind of died—just like that, and 'Baby-Killer' and Andre got back together. They left for France about a year ago."

But there are also some very touching manifestations of this passion. Joe tells me of a conversation with Pholla that has him almost choking back tears. "I was waiting at the school for Pholla to get there from the market so we could go home together. I was talking with one of the local teachers, this Chinese-Khmer, so when we get home, I'm expecting another round of jealousy. Instead, Pholla looks at me seriously and says, 'you should marry someone like that teacher.' She's saying, you know, 'her skin is so light, not black like me, and she has an education. She's better for you, she's a virgin, and you should marry a virgin, especially a virgin with an education. I know you won't marry me, I'm too black and I'm not a virgin and have no education. What I want is that when you have children, you'll hire me to take care of them. I love you and that'd be the best way to be near you and help you, and I'd be great with your kids.'"

Abandonment of Khmer women by their husbands is so severe because of the high value placed on female virginity. A 'proper' (read, virgin) Khmer woman who is not married is very difficult to talk to, much less date casually. Jeff, for example, teaches a neighbor of his in exchange for laundry service. The family is pleased that she is learning and are very friendly. But they never let Jeff inside the house when she is there. Their lessons must be conducted outside in the court-yard where everyone can see that there is no hanky-panky.

There will not be even the appearance of the thought of a hint of sexual contact until she is properly married. A Khmer proverb sums up this attitude; "Boys are like diamonds and girls are like cotton." When you drop a diamond in the mud, you can wash it, and it will still be perfect. Cotton that is sullied, however, can never regain its original purity.

In addition to her 'shameful' state as a non-virgin, Pholla also feels vulnerable because of her relatively dark skin color, as reflected in her "black like me" comment. Rachel, an NGO employee who does not frequent the Majestic, explains that, "I've given up trying to persuade Khmer women to be proud of their skin color. For them it's simple. Light skin is more attractive than dark skin. I can talk all I want about internalized racism or the lingering effects of European colonialism, but there's nothing I can do to make them see dark skin as anything but ugly.

"So, the markets are full of all these lotions that supposedly lighten your skin. They rub the cream in their faces before they go to bed. If they have more money to spare, they run the lotion into their arms as well. As if it wasn't bad enough that they spend their last dollars on this rubbish, a lot of the lower-quality ones are actually harmful. They weaken the skin, and make it more prone to scratches and scarring. And they avoid the sun like they're vampires. You've seen them walk along the street and they use anything—books, a hat, a scarf, anything, to shield their faces."

. As with everything else, this facet of Cambodian culture is, inevitably, associated with sex during conversations at the Majestic. It also provides an unfortunately perfect metaphor for too much of the Khmer-foreign interaction of the past few hundred years. Because Khmers, by their nature, tend not to be devious, this leaves a certain naiveté which unscrupulous foreigners—be they Vietnamese, Chinese, Malaysian, or American—can prey on. Dirk, the English teacher with long experience in Cambodia, gleefully explains the ease with which Khmers can be duped by manipulating their attitude toward skin color. "Hey, I finally figured out how to get Khmer girls to give blowjobs," he announces one day over lunch.

"Khmer women all think Viet Nam girls beautiful because they so light-skin, but disgusting because they so give blowjobs. Well, I just tell them Viet Nam girls are light-skin *because* they so give blowjobs. And the goddam Khmers believe it, and can't wait to start sucking."

In a healthier example of Khmer-foreign interaction, Joe confirms that Pholla does indeed use a lightening lotion. "It's pretty difficult to get excited about making love at night when your girlfriend's face is this pasty white and smells like hand lotion. But she's convinced that if she stops using it, I'll dump her for someone lighter skinned."

Given that Pholla is not a prostitute, I ask Joe about how they met. Over a couple of conversations, Joe gives me the full story of meeting Pholla. Besides just the logistical details of the beginning of their romance, Joe's tale provides a broad look at various facets of life among the Khmers. I present the entire story here (from Joe's point of view) in edited, paraphrased, journal form.

Roongkasal (Nightclub)
May 3, 1997

A smiling middle-aged man with just a touch of paunch is walking out as we are nearing the entrance. He is joking with the attendant at a small structure which looks like a state fair ticket booth. The jovial man is handed a long silver machine pistol from the ticket booth, takes a few steps away from the booth, lines his sights, and fires three shots into the night sky. "Yeah, still works," he chuckles to the weapons attendant.

My host, Peab, is non-plussed as he leads me towards the entrance. In a bizarre twist, I, a foreigner, am frisked for weapons while my Khmer companion is waved through, despite the fact that he is carrying a handgun (as he normally does). We are walking down a long series of wide wooden steps towards a huge barge moored at the side of the river. A flashing light display that could hold its head up high in Las Vegas announces, in English letters, that we are ap-

proaching the Chaktamok Floating Dancing Restaurant. Three other barges, similarly huge and similarly draped in lights, are lined up along the waterfront. There are working girls leaning against, and sitting on, the railing of the staircase down to the riverbank, as well as on the deck of the boat. They are all Khmers under 25-years-old, and maybe three quarters are teenagers. Most are quite stunning. They are smartly dressed, sexy but not necessarily slutty, and go for $20 to $40 per night, depending on the beauty of the girl and the wealth of the customer. Given that Tool Kok offers $2 alternatives, these sums are quite a premium for the 'class' of a nightclub girl.

We walk down the stairs, up the gangplank, then into the dance hall. In contrast to the visible-from-space light display outside, the dance hall is completely dark. It takes a few seconds for my eyes to adjust, but eventually I can make out a huge room, about half the size of a football field, crowded with tables and customers. The dance floor is small in comparison; about the size of a living room—plus half again for the band's raised stage. The room is pitch dark because we arrived during a sloo dance. This is the Khmer appropriation of 'slow dance' and is exactly what you did at junior high school birthday parties.

One of the most wonderful aspects of many Khmer love songs is that in between two of the verses, where Western musicians might put a guitar solo, the singer will literally sob into the microphone as the music plays in the background; ". . . oh baby {sniff}, when you left me, I . . . {choking sob} I thought I would die {sniff}. I will . . . {sob, sniff} I will always love you, and . . . {sob} never forget you . . ." And then on to the next verse. It is corny and exaggerated but strangely effective.

My appreciation of the music is interrupted by a waiter shining a small flashlight who leads us to our seats. Immediately, a host of 'marketing representatives' from different beer companies swarm to the table, inviting us to order their particular brand of beer. These women are young and pretty (though not as young as the prostitutes) and are employed by the beer companies to promote their brands in nightclubs and restaurants. Each company has its own uniform, from Tiger Beer's modern dark blue jumper and yellow vest, to Angkor Beer's classic Khmer dress, which is just tight enough to be sexy.

After we order our beers, Peab asks if we should order a girl as well. This can be arranged through a nightclub employee, or can be done independently. Either way, as soon as a nightclub girl sits at your table, you are liable for what is straightforwardly called a "girl charge." This is between $4 and $6 at most of the nightclubs, and appears right on your bill. I still remember my surprise on first seeing such a bill. It read simply,

Beer	$4
Juice	$2
Girl	$4

This money goes to the house, with the girl getting a percentage, and covers only time spent at your table, and dancing. Any further activity is negotiated independently between the two parties.

The question of a table companion is deferred because the dance floor suddenly lights up for the ram wong. The music, unlike anything commonly heard in the West, is perhaps best described as Islamic or Jewish prayer chants mixed with calypso music. Dancing to it is as beautiful as it is simple. The foot movements are basically slow, small steps around a circle. But the real action is in the hands; you move them up and down, curling and uncurling your fingers, turning the palms inward and outwards, and rotating at the wrists. Depending on the song, these actions are performed at a different pace, but always incredibly gracefully. With the disco lights, the music, and the sight of all of these men (at least a few of whom had to check their grenades or pistols at the door) and women (who, when they dance, define the meaning of grace) moving around in a circle as they wave and rotate their hands, I feel an intoxication that has nothing to do with the small amount of beer I have sipped so far.

All too soon, the music cycle rotates to disco, and we sit down. The playlist seems to run for about 10–15 minutes each of sloo, ram wong, and disco. Between ram wongs, Peab is chatting up a beer girl, and he calls for a nightclub girl to sit and keep me company. Sovanna, as she is called, is, of course, young and beautiful—and she adapts to speaking clearly so that I can follow.

An hour passes pleasantly; beer is consumed, the ram wong is danced, Sovanna teaches me some Thai she picked up in her home province in the Northwest, and Peab and the beer girl are laughing away. At 11:00, Peab calls for the check. He apologizes to Sovanna for leaving her unemployed for however long it takes for her to pick up another customer, but softens the blow with a generous tip. We head out back up the stairs towards Peab's car. Peab is an army officer, and his nominal salary is just over $63 per month. His $20,000 Toyota is either the result of careful saving of his salary for the past 26 years, or is a consequence of corruption in the Royal Cambodian Armed Forces. I know that he is stationed in an area of the country where there is illegal logging, but I inquire no further than that.

We wait in his car for a minute and the beer girl he was talking to appears as well. At $40 a month, beer girls' salaries are comparable to those of army officers. This sum, plus occasional tips, makes it possible to get by, but hardly live comfortably. Many live with their families, and so have no expenses to speak of. Others supporting themselves often end up 'adopted' as a mistress by someone like Peab. I soon find out that this has been the case with Pholla, who, for the past couple of months, has been Peab's part-time plaything.

We are nearing my house, and I am ready to be simply dropped off. The Khmers are certainly a hospitable bunch. Last week when Peab and I went out, we retired to his house for some drinks after the nightclub closed. At about 1:00 am, I told him I should be going home. Mentioning the late hour, he pulled out a pistol from his waistband and asked if I would like to borrow it for the ride home. Tonight, instead of offering me his pistol, he offers me his mistress. As I understood it last week, he was to lend me his pistol; but the mistress, he now wants to transfer to me outright. "She can be your girlfriend and wash your clothes and clean your room and cook for you. All you have to do is keep her fed and housed," he says, as if explaining the obvious. Pholla, meanwhile, begins crying quietly in the back seat—I guess this is as much a shock to her as it is to me.

Although this is certainly the most exceptional 'gift' anyone has ever offered to me, I find that I am not yet Khmer enough to accept it. Lying to Peab, I explain that although Pholla is quite lovely, I have a girlfriend abroad. In order not to disappoint him, as he is so eager to find a friend for his mistress and mistress for his friend, I suggest that I hire Pholla to cook and clean, and that with the salary, she can rent a place to live. Although he is confused by my strange reaction, Peab seems satisfied that at least a partial solution has been found. Pholla, still sniffling, manages a brave smile. As I notice once again how pretty she is, I realize that I should get out of the car before I change my mind.

"I'll bring her by tomorrow at noon," Peab promises. I thank him, nod good-bye to Pholla, and step out of the car. I shut the door firmly, as if confirming my decision not to take up Peab's offer of a lover as well as a maid. Standing at the gate outside my yard, I watch as the car disappears into the darkness of Phnom Penh.

So I did hire her, and it worked out well. We got to know each other, and I found I really liked her. So I ended up taking Peab up on his offer after all. It was a strange beginning, but we have a strong relationship now. When she's not hysterically accusing me of infidelity, she's pleasantly quick to laugh. Although her education and knowledge of the world are a bit lacking, she is smart and curious. As I tell the guys when they ask about our relationship, "She's the nicest present anyone has ever given me. Now I know what I should have asked for for my birthday all those years." Recently, Pholla confessed to me that she didn't love me when we first got together. But, she says, when she saw that I was "kind" and could take care of her, she came to love me "truly a lot."

Coup

The timing of my July trip to Cambodia is impeccable. I left Saigon Friday morning, July 4, and arrived in Phnom Penh late that evening. There was a hold up at the border as a motorcade coming from Viet Nam crossed into Cambodia. I find out later that it was Hun Sen returning from one of his occasional unannounced overland trips to Viet Nam. "To pick up his paycheck," jokes Joe. Since I expect that this will be my last trip to Cambodia, I have rented a motorbike in order to do some exploring on my own. Later in the morning, I meet up with Joe, who updates me on the deteriorating political situation. Recently, rumors have been flying that the Khmer Rouge forces are ready to stop their continued insurgence and join the government, on Ranaridh's side. This could affect the military balance of power, although it is unclear exactly to what extent. In addition, tensions soared over a three-ton shipment of weapons, labeled "spare parts," that Ranaridh brought into the country for his bodyguard unit (private army). Things have been simmering ever since the grenade attack on March 30. There was even a brief firefight in the city in mid-June.

Still, we are all surprised when the first shells start falling in the late afternoon. Although they sound distant, there is already a sense of panic in the air. People are driving hastily, hurrying to get home to loved ones. The Khmers have an overdeveloped sense of caution concerning civil unrest; understandable given their catastrophic recent history. I remember Steve describing how a student explained her absence from class for that tense week after the grenade attack; "She said, 'I was at a friend's house when the Khmer Rouge came to Phnom Penh. Everybody was evacuated and I wasn't with my family. I never saw my father or uncles again. So now when things are tense, I just don't leave home.'"

I feel a kind of strange excitement going about my casual shopping to the sounds of shellfire. But all the stores are shutting their doors anyway, so I head back to the Majestic. Joe and Pholla are in the middle of an early dinner. As the shelling intensifies, Joe tells me that Pholla is frantic. "She's really worried we might be separated, begging me to stay with her. She also says we should pack one bag each so we have something ready to take in case they evacuate the city 'like last time.' Then she starts telling me about when the Khmer Rouge took the city and everyone had to leave for the countryside, so we'd better have a bag ready just in case. I'm trying not to roll my eyes or laugh. There's no telling her that Pol Pot isn't on his way to evacuate the city." Joe imitates her high-pitched frenzy; "'What do you know. You were in New Zealand. I was just a little baby, but I remember last time how we all had to leave right away.' There's no way I can convince her she's overreacting."

Reiner joins us at the table. He just had a long talk with one of his many Khmer business partners who told him that, "The CPP have the FUNCINPEC guys surrounded. They're not actually going at them full force, they're firing mostly into the air or into the defense perimeter. They want to force a surrender rather than launch a full scale attack. Also, you know how Hun Sen spent the last four days in Viet Nam? My partner says that thousands of Vietnamese troops are massed at the border, ready to come in if Hun Sen needs help. They'd use the excuse of protecting Vietnamese civilians from Khmer Rouge massacres. He said that if they had to, the CPP would massacre some Vietnamese themselves to provide the excuse. By the way, there's a curfew on from eight tonight to six am."

It's just coming on 6:00 pm now, and we turn on the BBC World Service to find out what is going on. With the sounds of shells falling outside, the big news on the BBC is that there is a problem with the Pathfinder space mission to Mars. Reiner tries to tune into any of the local stations. The FUNCINPEC station is off the air but he stops at another station broadcasting a speech by Hun Sen. Listening to Hun Sen angrily rail away, Reiner translates what he can. "He keeps talking about illegal weapons and the Khmer Rouge brought to the city by Ranaridh. He says it's not a coup but he had to use force to prevent a coup by Ranaridh using the illegal weapons and KR troops."

"Classic CPP," says Joe. "They do something and then accuse the other side of it." Reiner changes the station. "This is interesting. It's a guy appealing to the FUNCINPEC soldiers to surrender. He says they shouldn't die for their leaders who are all outside the country 'sleeping and eating delicious food.'" Reiner turns the radio off, and we sit and listen to the booms of the shells and the cracks of the gunfire. As it begins to get dark, the firing becomes less intense. I sit on the balcony, listening to the intermittent sounds of battle. The streets are empty and quiet. The curfew hour approaches and the firing dies down to nothing. There is no place I particularly want to go, but it is still frustrating to be housebound. This is my first experience under curfew, and I resent the lack of freedom. But the fact that everyone is indoors has an unexpected benefit. For the first time in my entire Phnom Penh experience, there is quiet outside—no traffic noise, no ice cream sellers, just a very peaceful calm. With a beer from the restaurant downstairs and a sci-fi book from my travel bag, I go back to the porch to read.

At 9:00 pm, we learn from the radio that NASA mission control is close to fixing the problems with the Pathfinder mission.

Phnom Penh at War
July 6, 1997

I wake up early the next morning, as do the soldiers. We hear some firing, but it seems to be just a warm-up. I go out

to the balcony and look around. There is a fair amount of traffic—although nothing close to usual, and a sense of urgency
in the drivers. The motorbike I rented is just about out of gas,
so filling it up is my first priority. The filling station closest to
the guesthouse is closed, but across the street from it is one
of the many sidewalk vendors who sell gasoline out of one
and two liter glass soda bottles. The scene is straight out of
The Road Warrior, as people clamor around the vendor trying to buy the last drops of gasoline. The price I keep hearing, 5,000 riel per liter, is roughly four times the usual price of
1,300. The vendor is completely sold out by the time I shout
for a liter. I kick-start my motorbike, but to no avail—the tank
is as dry as the gasoline stand next to me.

Abandoning the bike, I go on foot to the gasoline stand I
hope is around the corner. Here too, I see panic buying, and
the price has risen to 6,000 riel, but I manage to get a hold of
the last liter of priceless gas. In this situation I can leave my
motorbike unattended, but no way will I let the gasoline out
of my sight. Borrowing the bottle, I walk to the bike and fill it.
Only then do I return the bottle and collect my change.

With the gas taken care of, I am able to focus on my surroundings. A large plume of black smoke is rising up above
the city to the west—the direction of the airport. Closer in, I
see family after family with their precious few belongings fleeing the city. Some are on cyclos, some are on foot, others are
pulling small wagons containing everything they own. They
all look poor and frightened and pathetic.

I head to the guesthouse to plan out the rest of the day.
Suddenly the manager rushes upstairs and says something
to me in Khmer about "gasoline" and "motorbike." I go downstairs to find that my gas tank is leaking. All the gasoline I
struggled so hard to obtain is lying on the tile of the court-
yard. I recall that someone abandoned a motorbike here yesterday. It is the same make as mine, so there is a good chance
my key will work. Then I remember that he left it here because it too, ran out of gas. I remain just as immobile as before, so I head upstairs to listen to the shells explode. Steve
comes out of his room grinning like a Cheshire cat. He has

just returned from a long vacation in Laos and, after three days of Tool Kok, Svay Pa, discos, and drugs, he has settled in with a girl from Champagne while Lan is in Viet Nam. "Well, she's a little cutie," he says, rubbing his hands. "Her house is near FUNCINPEC HQ, so she's staying here until the fighting ends. Personally, I hope it's a long, drawn out battle."

Reiner turns up with a radio broadcasting a speech by Hun Sen. His coarse voice, crude at the best of times, sounds ragged, vitriolic, and not quite lucid—deranged even. He is slurring his words as he spits rhetoric into the microphone. Reiner translates what he can. "He keeps using the word 'traitor.' 'Ranaridh is a traitor to his country, and to the people of Cambodia, and to his party.' And he keeps calling him 'Ranaridh'— not 'Prince' or 'First Prime Minister', or even 'Mr.', just Ranaridh, Ranaridh. There it is again, 'Ranaridh the traitor.'"

I go back to the patio to listen to the shells and wait for something to happen. It is a warm sunny day, and the patio is a pleasant and comfortable place from which to witness civil unrest. A group of soldiers fans out from the CPP compound across the intersection. They are followed by first one, then a second massive armored personnel carrier. The APCs and the soldiers set up a roadblock at the far end of the intersection, close to their base. The immediate vicinity of the Majestic is quiet, and the soldiers are taking a fairly relaxed approach to their defense perimeter. Nevertheless, it is disconcerting to have combatants within sight and within gunfire range of my porch.

The morning wears on. At about 11:00, the shelling and firing start to die down. By half past, the fighting stops altogether—for what is apparently a lunch-break cease-fire. Now seems a good time to scout around. Moving slowly out of the guesthouse, I approach the soldiers on the corner with a big smile. They smile back and ask for, or is it demand, a light for their cigarettes. Whichever, I figure that I can afford to spare a light for these teenagers with guns. I tell them to wait a moment and, from my room, I bring a matchbook from Vertigo—a restaurant in Pittsburgh where I went out for my last meal before leaving the US for Viet Nam. Vertigo's matches are soon firing up the cigarettes of Hun Sen's boy soldiers during a coup in Phnom Penh.

The main roads in front of the guesthouse are blocked by CPP troops to prevent civilians moving around, but the smaller streets out back are open. There is very little traffic. A couple of moto drivers proposition me with outrageous fare requests. It is a beautiful, sunny day, and ironically—considering the circumstances, I am enjoying the stroll along the quiet streets cleared of traffic. I walk around the Royal Palace, and into the vicinity of Prince Ranaridh's residence. On a far corner, an APC is maneuvering into position, so I turn down another street. As I round the corner, I see a study in contrasts; a huge army officer, his flak jacket bursting with grenades that expand his already bulky frame, is talking to a wisp of an old man walking a bicycle. To the old man's request for permission to walk down the street, the soldier answers curtly, "Sure you can walk down there, if you don't mind dying. They're about to start killing each other."

This is as close as I want to get to combat journalism, so I turn for home. On the way, I meet a family sitting outside enjoying the lunchtime cease-fire. We chat, and I am asked for the millionth time if I'm not afraid and if I'm going back to my country. Later in the conversation, they also mention gasoline being sold in the southern part of the city. Moving on, I pass a group of moto drivers close to the guesthouse who invite me to join them on a gas run. One of the drivers grabs a jerrycan, and I hold it as we make our way down the open back roads to the city's south side. In these back alleys of the Bo Din shanty area, life is going on almost as usual, with the alley-stores open and traffic moving about the muddy streets.

On the way to the gas station, we pass the sprawling CPP headquarters. As an unnecessary precaution, they have stationed two mammoth APCs to guard the compound. Some soldiers are sunning themselves on the roofs of the vehicles, while their comrades sit in beach chairs in the shade that these tanks provide. We procure the gasoline without incident, and the driver brings me close to the guesthouse so I can fill up the motorbike. The soldiers on the corner are not happy to *see us, and there are some tense moments as they make their displeasure known by pointing their guns at us. The driver quickly turns the moto around. I dismount and approach on foot, slowly. I explain that I want to go back to fill my bike and then return the rest of the gas to the waiting moto driver. They give permission and I fill up my empty but functional motorbike, return the jerrycan, and go back upstairs, suddenly exhausted. Moving around during a civil war is much more tiring than I expected.*

The coup is mostly boredom. For those outside the main areas of action it means sitting around listening to the intermittent crescendos of gun and rocket fire. But our little upheaval has finally knocked the Pathfinder mission off the top of the BBC's news broadcasts. Steve and his "little cutie" come up for air occasionally, and every so often Reiner gives me a translation of news or propaganda he hears on the radio. Henrik is euphoric. For so long he has only dreamt about war and gunfire. I joke that he has been waiting for this eruption in Cambodia's political tension for a long time. "All my life," he responds.

Towards late afternoon, the shelling and firing slacken off, and by evening have all but stopped. Reiner tells us that the radio has announced that the fighting is over, and everyone should return to their normal lives tomorrow. The day ends with a group of us sitting in the Majestic chatting about the KR, the future of Cambodia, and shagging.

Fear and Looting in Phnom Penh
July 7, 1997

On waking up, I go out to the porch to assess the situation. There are no sounds of firing, no plumes of smoke, and no soldiers in evidence. Traffic, though lighter than usual, is noisily present. During breakfast, there is a moment of tension when one solitary shell explodes in the morning calm. In the long silence that follows, I decide to explore the city.

The first stop is FUNCINPEC headquarters. The building bears the scars of heavy fighting. The letters on the sign are

askew, bullet holes pockmark the entire length of the compound, and there is a hole perhaps one yard in diameter
punched into the perimeter wall. The whole area is patrolled
and guarded by troops. Unlike the soldiers near the guesthouse, who identified themselves with white strips of cloth
tied to their shoulder straps or guns, these guys display red
strips. Hope clouding reason, I wonder if white is for CPP and
red for FUNCINPEC, and that FUNCINPEC troops somehow
managed to repulse the assault. I stop my motorbike in front
of a group of soldiers to inquire.

The first thing I notice is their age—maybe 16 or 17-years-
old. The second thing I notice is the greedy grins on their faces.
The first armed and uniformed teenager I approach quickly
confirms that they are CPP troops. Then he asks to borrow
the motorbike; "Just for a short ride. Let me try it out." A
second adolescent approaches. "He'll bring it back," he lies. I
pretend to have misunderstood, and say, "Sure, hop on and I
can give you a ride." A third armed teenager tries a different
tack. "Give us some money. Twenty dollars." I give them the
same disappointed smile I would give if my best friend suddenly asked me to help him steal a car. "Naw, I can't do that,"
I say in a conciliatory, apologetic tone. Before the situation
has a chance to escalate a 'senior' teenager with a gun waves
me off. Relieved, I drive away.

The second stop on my itinerary is the airport. I head down
the main airport road just to confirm my assumption that it is
roadblocked. Indeed it is—by a tank. I decide to circle around
and try a back road to the airport. I have to pause briefly while
traffic is stopped to allow another tank to cross the street, but
I am soon cruising down the road to the southwestern part of
the city.

The home of Nhiek Bun Chai is in this area, and his
neighborhood is where all the fighting began. Nhiek Bun Chai
was the man most instrumental in bringing the Khmer Rouge
into the government fold (on FUNCINPEC's side) and thus
provoking Hun Sen's violent preemptive action. The
neighborhood where he lives—lived—has two main 'en-
trances' onto the main boulevard. I approach one of them to

find a large crowd of Khmers standing opposite the entry road. There is a roadblock preventing the residents from entering their own neighborhood—while the soldiers are moving in and out freely. A bystander says, "Tee-ya-hee-un kompong yo roboh brojee-ya-joon." The soldiers are taking—he does not use the Khmer word for stealing—the things of the people. He continues in Khmer, "They won the battle, so now they are taking the things that are in the houses. They are taking the things that belong to the people in the houses."

I spend a long time at this entrance, and at an identical show at the other. Pairs of soldiers ride out on motorbikes with TVs in between them, while others walk out with radios and other electrical appliances. An army jeep, with a makeshift tow line of sheets, hauls a car away. A couple of trucks roll by loaded with refrigerators, motorbikes, fans, anything that wasn't nailed down. Nothing is left behind. One bystander even identifies his bedsheets being carried out by a passing soldier. An APC lumbers by with several fans strapped on behind its huge roof-mounted machine gun.

The Khmers I speak with are furious but powerless, and they are pleased that I am taking pictures of the looting. "If there are no pictures, they will say we are lying," says one. "But now people will believe us." Another laments that, "Everything I worked for is gone. They took everything." A Western journalist I meet says that the airport has been completely stripped; "They even towed away the RAC minibuses." The Khmers have a saying that when elephants fight, only ants die. Here, I am watching one of the elephants scooping up what little possessions the ants have. The ants can only stand and watch, and hope that they will have better luck in their next lives.

Eventually, I tire of watching the army steal from its own people. From the main road, I turn off onto a dirt side road and make for the airport. As expected, the road is blocked. But something is wrong here. It is not an established barrier, but rather gun-and-rocket-toting teenagers who are moving forward, clearing people from their path at gunpoint. These civilians look panic-stricken as they rush toward and past me. Unlike the teenage soldiers in town who are generally good-

humored, these advancing troops look ready to kill at the slightest excuse. I get a very bad feeling. As I turn my motorbike around, it stalls in the mud—a common occurrence, but at an uncommonly bad time. I try the kick-start a few times, but it refuses to start. For the first time since the shells first started bursting, I feel scared; not once-in-a-lifetime adventurous, not-wait-'til-I-tell-'em-back-home excited, but truly afraid of dying. Taking a deep breath, and ready to abandon the motorbike to the advancing soldiers, I finally get it started. Spooked, I make my way to the Majestic for lunch.

I couldn't verify what was happening in this situation at the time, but I later worked out theories after consulting with journalists and knowledgeable residents. One, they were CPP-allied KR troops who only recently left the jungle, and/or, two, they were transporting either prisoners or corpses of massacred FUNCINPEC/FUNCINPEC-allied KR soldiers.

There is a big group in the restaurant, providing a perfect chance to exchange information and rumors. Mike says he heard that the airport road opened late in the morning, and that there are some burned out tanks on the way. He also heard two more worrying rumors. According to the first one, a Khmer-Canadian was shot dead while photographing soldiers. The story was explicit; he was shot in the leg, then he threw away the camera, then he pleaded in English (because he did not speak Khmer), then he was shot in the head. The second rumor is about an Englishman beaten up and robbed by two soldiers. In a story eerily reminiscent of my experience this morning, the Englishman was driving two soldiers around. One of them stuck his hand inside the Englishman's pocket to get the wallet. When he resisted, the soldiers beat him and took the money and the bike.[1]

After a quick lunch, Mike and I head out for the airport. The main road is indeed open now. At one of the main intersections along the road, standing directly under an enormous ABC Stout billboard, are the charred remains of a tank. Every

---

[1] The first rumor was substantiated later, but I was never able to confirm the second one.

square inch is scorched black. Around the corner is a tank in even worse shape. The turret has been blown completely off and is lying on the ground about a meter away, with the barrel lodged into the ground. People are climbing on the body of the tank and peering inside, examining the torn metal which looks like the violently exposed innards of some great metallic beast. I am hopping about photographing the wreckage when Mike points to an unexploded tank shell only a few inches from my feet.

The road to the airport is replete with similar, if less dramatic, evidence of the fighting. There are bullet and shell holes in walls, fences and windows. The road itself is etched with the marks of tank treads, and we can see where they have turned themselves around, either to engage an enemy in the rear, or stage a tactical retreat. We travel onward to see a pair of tank treads lying in the middle of the road. The tank itself is nowhere to be seen.

The shops and factories along the road are mostly deserted, but there is some activity at the enormous Jeep Cambodia center. Locals are climbing onto the warehouse roof and prying off sheets of corrugated metal. Mike rightly points out that instead of stealing a few cents worth of metal, they could rob us. Our pocket change alone is one or two months salary for many of these looters. And yet, there is some kind of code of conduct here in the chaos; plundering deserted sites is apparently acceptable, but armed robbery is not.

Moving on, we see the familiar sight of the airport gates. The airport is quiet and empty, except for groups of mean-looking soldiers. The place is completely uninviting, and we continue past.

We stop to watch the activity at a nearby auxiliary building which houses the company that runs the airport. It is being thoroughly ransacked. The soldiers, having finished their own looting, are now selling 'concessions' to civilians; as they exit the compound with their haul, each civilian has to pay the soldiers at the gate a commission based on the value of their loot. It is a testimony to human greed and perseverance to watch an 80-year-old woman steal a file cabinet easily twice *her size. She struggles to place it precariously on a rickety old bicycle and manages to pedal off toward home. Mike and I watch as the locals strew the maintenance records, personnel records, and blueprints of the airport management company all over the ground as they load up their motorbikes and bicycles with file cabinets and desk drawers.*

"When in Rome . . ." I think as I slowly approach the soldiers at the gate. They do not seem bothered by my presence, so I continue in. A shot rings out behind me, but I have enough experience in Cambodia to know that it is probably nothing more than a greeting. I turn around with a friendly questioning expression. A soldier has his AK-47 pointed at the sky and is smiling at me. The shot is just to remind me that he is armed and I am not. "Can I go in?" I ask. "Ot banyaha," (no problem) says the smiling marksman. I acknowledge his permission and turn around, ready to be worried only if there is another shot.

At the building itself, people are hard at work removing the metal grates in front of the windows, and then the window panes themselves. One ambitious man is trying to pry out an air-conditioning unit. I manage to find a storeroom with all sorts of detritus, ironically including a portrait of the King draped in Cambodian flags. I grab the flags and also a large sign in English and Khmer announcing PASSENGERS ONLY, and head back outside, wondering on what basis I will negotiate the theft fee with the soldiers. But it is unnecessary as they lackadaisically wave me through the gate. Mike laughs at my sign, but agrees to carry it on the way home.

Although the curfew has been lifted, people are worried about increased lawlessness and are simply staying indoors after dark. I follow the trend of retiring early.

Aftermath
July 8, 1997

Jeff, Steve, and I are all up early for another trip to the airport. We stop at the same battle scenes as yesterday to

163

give Jeff and Steve a chance to take a look. When we arrive at the airport, the gates are closed but completely unguarded, making it easy enough to slip inside. The parking lot is empty except for a couple of cars. We pass a bowling ball lying on the ground—perhaps a looter got frustrated with its weight and abandoned it. A water truck outside the terminal has a large rocket hole in its front windshield. From the front, though, the terminal building itself does not look damaged.

Once we get inside, however, I am shocked by the destruction. It is the world's rowdiest frat party gone berserk; empty liquor bottles from the duty free shop, boxes and papers, and broken glass all over the place. All of the fixtures and fittings have been stripped. But there is no gunfire damage that we can see; this was all done by human hands. We wander around, marveling at the thoroughness of the looting. Not only have the check-in counters of Royal Air Cambodge been stripped of all the computers, but even the pens have been taken. All the drawers have been ripped out and emptied onto the floor to make sure that nothing of value escaped. I now understand the difference between stealing and looting. Besides just looking for valuables, Hun Sen's soldiers were celebrating their victory with a wild rampage of drunken destruction. Wading through the wreckage, I notice a book lying amid the debris; the title is Cambodia: A Portrait.

The devastation bothers me, but Jeff is distraught. He taught RAC classes through his school, and he got to know many of the airline's personnel. He leads us through a smashed door into an office littered with paper. "I remember talking with the manager in this very office about training," says Jeff. "Now look at it." He starts sifting through the binders randomly thrown across the floor. "Here," he says, handing me the binder. It contains a series of memos he wrote about the classes.

We work our way through the devastation to the runway side of the terminal. One section of the terminal building carries very significant battle damage. The ceiling of one area is now nothing but concrete confetti on the ground. We see bullet holes in windows and walls, and whole sections of wall ripped apart—the metal struts inside twisted painfully. As dramatic as it is in these sections, however, the overall structural damage to the terminal building looks minimal.

I spot a group of Frenchmen being escorted around by some soldiers, and I tag along as if I belong. I am led, unimpeded by anyone, up into the control tower of the airport. There are some bullet holes in one of the windows, but the control room seems to have escaped otherwise intact. There is a crowd of men hard at work bringing a Thai Air Force transport plane out of the sky as I snap pictures. Finally, for the first time all day, someone (politely) asks me to leave.

I meet up with Steve and Jeff again down on the tarmac. The Thai planes—Steve points out two more circling above— are here to evacuate Thai nationals. In contrast to the ease with which I wandered onto the runway, the Thais are massed behind a gate, waiting their turn for evacuation. Soon there is a line of Thais on the tarmac. The moment the huge back doors of the first giant C-130 open, the Thais are urged forward to fill up the plane. Even though there is no evident danger, everything is done at emergency pacing, and the effect is quite (melo)dramatic. There are tough-looking, sunglass-clad Thai commandos with submachine guns at the ready, standing back to back guarding the entrance to the planes. White gloved-commandos bring the panicking Thais scurrying toward the loading bay. When one transport begins filling up, another gets into position, and the Thais are directed, running, to the appropriate plane. It is easy to get caught up in the emotion of it, especially when one of the commandos runs forward carrying a little baby onto the plane.

Jeff and I head over to inspect the RAC aircraft. As we circle the plane, Jeff tells me that RAC has two Boeing 737 jets and three ATR-72 propeller planes. One of his students reported that one of the Boeings was en route from Malaysia, but turned back on news of the fighting. It sat out the coup in the hands of Malaysian Airlines, a 40% owner of RAC. The other Boeing is in front of us. Surprisingly, given the wholesale looting inside the terminal, the jet looks completely unscathed. We accompany a Malaysian (we assume) engineer as he inspects the plane's engines and landing gear. As he goes up the stairs to inspect the avionics inside, I try to board with him, but am turned back.

We make another sweep inside the terminal. This time, Steve collects a spent bullet lodged inside a ream of customs forms. I help myself to a Malaysian Airlines Transit Passenger pass as well as a Malaysian Airlines Firearms Carriage pass, just in case I might need them someday. Tired and thirsty, we head for home.

On the way back, we stop at the intersection of the burned out tanks. Policemen and soldiers are clearing the area of traffic and setting up roadblocks. The charred tank (the whole one) is to be towed away. The soldiers all seem nervous that the tank will explode when moved, so Steve and I take cover behind a wooden desk. We have a great view, as the tank is just across the road.

A special tow-tank is brought in and cabled to the dead beast. It chugs away, but cannot dislodge its immobile brother, so another tank is summoned and attached to the tow-tank. As Steve and I crouch behind the desk, the two tanks—in tandem—manage just barely to get the third one rolling. We watch the ungainly parade of metal rumble off. Luckily, we never found out just how little protection an old desk affords from an exploding tank ten yards away.

We get back without further incident. I have a long, late lunch at the Majestic, and then a leisurely, relaxed afternoon. To celebrate surviving four days of coup and adventure, Joe, Steve, and I go to an Indian restaurant. Darkness has fallen by the time we head home. As I drive down the familiar stretch of road, a car suddenly shoots straight for us while passing another car. Only by swerving out of the way do I avoid death. This brush with disaster underscores the wisdom of getting home before dark. It looks like things are going to be unsettled for the time being.

Journey

Upon returning to Viet Nam after the July coup in Phnom Penh, I decided that that trip to Cambodia would be my last. It would have been too easy to convince myself of the need to do more 'field research' about the brothels, the lakeside pot-houses, and the firing range. I could see the effect Cambodia had on her residents, and I was eager to keep myself on the tamer side of existence.

With my research in Cambodia finished, and my basic credentials in business journalism established, I was ready to find steady employment. I managed to secure a job in Bangkok, which added an even greater sense of closure to the Cambodian adventure. After the oppressiveness and savage greed of Viet Nam and the shabbiness of Phnom Penh, modern Bangkok and the easygoing Thais were a welcome change. I was enjoying my first two months in Bangkok, right up until the time my new employer gave me a forced and unpaid one week vacation.

I decided to make the best of it and left Bangkok for the southeast corner of Thailand. Trat province has a sizable Khmer community and some relatively untouristed beaches. I spent the first day in Trat town trying to get information about crossing to Cambodia.

The general picture is that the land border at Hat Lek is open for Cambodians and Thais only. One can cross by sea, but it can be very difficult to return to Thailand. Because there

167

are no exit or entry stamps authorized for Hat Lek, the Thais are unwelcoming to anyone trying to enter there. Apparently, one can 'enter' Cambodia at Hat Lek only if one has never 'left' Thailand, i.e. you leave Thailand without an exit stamp, and receive no entry or exit stamps from Cambodia. I will try to enter Cambodia but avoid any Cambodian formalities which would mark my passport with evidence of my trip.

In high spirits, I leave Trat town. I am looking forward to the adventure, especially since saying, "I snuck across the border to Cambodia" sounds much more dangerous and exciting than it really is. Khlong Yai, the area's other main town, and Hat Lek beyond it, lie at the southeastern-most tip of Thailand on a very long and narrow sliver of land that juts out from the main body of Trat province. The Khmer nationalist in me is out-raged at whatever clever Siamese maneuvering allowed them to extend their coastline so far down into what was very obvi-ously once part of Cambodia's Koh Kong province.

Once in Khlong Yai, I start inquiring about a land crossing into Cambodia that will avoid the Hat Lek checkpoint. Over and over again I am told in Thai, Khmer, Chinese, and English that Hat Lek is the only crossing point. In this area, people explain, Cambodia and Thailand are separated by hills inhab-ited only by landmines and bandits. The only alternative even mentioned is a place called Khlong Soon. A Khmer-speaking motorcycle driver takes me there. Khlong Soon is a disap-pointing sight. I had expected some small village on the bor-der from which I could just stroll into Cambodia. Instead, I am standing on a pier looking out into the Gulf of Thailand.

The harbor is the perfect image of a Thai fishing town. Scruffy, dark men and women are shoveling shrimps from piles on the pier into packing crates, while small wooden fish-ing boats clutter alongside the jetties. As the only farang in town it doesn't take long before a Khmer speaker finds me (as opposed to vice versa) and I outline my plan to get to Cambodia. Eventually he finds another man, who comes over and tells me that he can take me on his fishing boat without going through Hat Lek, but not until the day after tomorrow, and not all the way to Koh Kong.

I decide to keep exploring my options. Besides the prospect of a long wait here or back in Trat town, safety is another factor. This area is full of smugglers, illegal loggers, bandits, and pirates—all of whom should be presumed armed. There has been significant Khmer Rouge activity in the recent past, and I also suspect that the provincial police and military are probably less predictable than their Bangkok or Phnom Penh counterparts. While a well-meaning but ignorant friend in Bangkok labeled my venture as "suicidal," I take a more realistic approach. Crossing into Cambodia is merely a matter of calculated risks. Sticking to well-trafficked areas and moving in daylight will reduce my risk of being robbed to a minimum, and my risk of being hurt to infinitesimal—certainly lower than riding a motorcycle taxi through Bangkok. Hiding in the hold of a fishing boat tramping through sparsely populated islands, however, seems to be tipping the scale toward unacceptable risk. In general, foreigners get into trouble in Cambodia either when resisting armed robbers or getting tangled with the Khmer Rouge. Because I am carrying nothing that I would hesitate to hand over, a robber will find me a most agreeable victim. By asking the locals about any Khmer Rouge activity, I can probably avoid that scene altogether. Overall, with a bit of good judgment, I believe my journey is much safer, and thus less adventurous, than most people would ever imagine.

Instead of the fishing boat, I try my luck at Hat Lek, a few minutes down the road. I smile at the Thai officials at the checkpoint. They smile in return, but explain that they simply cannot allow non-Thais or non-Cambodians to cross. Still smiling, I casually lean against the counter of their little shack, giving them every opportunity to change their minds or request a 'special fee.' They confer briefly. "No have way you exit here," one says apologetically, pointing to the gate that lies just between the hill and the sea. Then he points to the hill separating me from Cambodia and says, "Can go there, but you walk mine, we no can help you." Walking into Cambodia through the jungle would make a great story, but I am not ready to risk a leg for it. Resigned, I peer into Cambodia and then admire the Thai soldiers' heavy caliber machine gun pointing up at the hill I was just invited to cross.

The next attempt is by sea. Moored to a small pier near the land crossing is a flotilla of small plastic motorboats with 30 or 40 horsepower motors attached. Except for the Thai soldier strolling around, everyone on the pier speaks Khmer. They explain that it is impossible for me to go. With my motorbike driver as translator, I speak with the soldier. He laughingly tells me that, although it is illegal for me to exit Thailand, it is perfectly acceptable for me to get in a boat. I just need to remember that the Thais are not responsible for what happens if the boat I happen to get into leaves Thai waters. With that, the soldier walks off the pier.

Suddenly, going to Cambodia is as difficult as stepping into one of the motorboats. Joined by two Khmers and a Thai, we speed off along the coast. Within a couple of minutes, the Koh Kong International Resort Club comes into view. It is a huge casino built just inside Cambodian territory so that the gambling-addicted Thais can roll the dice without violating Thailand's anti-gaming laws. The rest of the half hour trip is a pleasant ride hugging the unpopulated coastline. The only distractions are identical speedboats making the trip in the other direction.

We make a turn around a ridge jutting out into the sea and I can see a small coastal settlement which turns out to be Koh Kong town. As we approach the shore, I see no officialdom at all—just a collection of motorboats moored along the beach, and a small market beyond. When we land on the beach, I hop out, make my way up to the market, and then on to the main road. I am back in Cambodia.

I spend some time wandering around, reminding myself of the overwhelming friendliness of the Khmers and the unrelenting shabbiness of their country. Koh Kong, capital of Cambodia's southwest—and tagged with the Khmer for "city"—is merely a comfortable little backwater town with fresh air and no buildings above two stories. I know about the large-scale illegal logging and smuggling that goes on in the region, but on the surface, Koh Kong is just a dusty, but pleasant, provincial seaside town.

The locals tell me of the town's only foreign resident, an English teacher from Canada named John. Within minutes of arriving in town, I am at his house, and he invites me to make myself at home for as long as I wish. John is an amicable, hospitable, and warm human being. Compared to the frenetic debauchery of the teachers in Phnom Penh, John's life is one of relaxed contentment. He teaches a couple of hours a day, plays music on his guitar, listens to loud music on his stereo, smokes ganja almost continuously, and stays faithful to his girlfriend in Canada who visits him every few months.

We talk about life in Koh Kong. The coup was a non-event here; if it had not been on the news, he would not have known about it. He tells me that, "Koh Kong is actually a FUNCINPEC province, but there's so much logging and smuggling that nobody wants to rock the boat just for ideology. I'm sure they just switched the guy they pay off in Phnom Penh to stay out of their hair and that's the end of it." While the areas far from town are infested with bandits, armed smugglers, and loggers, the town itself is a small community where there is very little crime. With so little nightlife, John is often in bed and asleep by 8 or 9 o'clock.

John also gives me tips about the border crossing. My wish to re-enter Thailand means that I cannot take the usual route to Phnom Penh—the boat to Sihanoukville—because that port city has a legitimate immigration office. Taking the boat means a stamp in my passport and thus problems with the Thais when I return.

I recall that RAC flies to Koh Kong, and have no difficulty finding their office in this one-horse town. The airline's staff, all three of them lounging about their office watching TV, inform me that there are two flights a week. To my inquiry, they tell me that neither a passport nor any immigration formalities are required for this internal flight. I hand over my $50 and receive my boarding pass for tomorrow's flight.

Off the Rails in Phnom Penh

My stamp-less journey to Phnom Penh settled, I return to John's house. Apart from a brief interlude when he is teaching, the rest of the day is spent smoking ganja, listening to music, and chatting about both of these topics.

Return to Phnom Penh
October 13, 1997

The ride out to the airport in the fresh morning air of the verdant countryside is brisk and invigorating. 'Airport,' however, is not quite an accurate title for this particular facility—even airfield is a charitable description for a landing strip, a gazebo, a shack, and a windsock. The shack is the police headquarters for the area and, inside, I unenthusiastically lie to the affable officers about how my passport is in Phnom Penh. They write down my name and passport number and send me to the gazebo which serves as the waiting area.

In short order, the turboprop ATR-72 arrives from Phnom Penh and disgorges its dozen passengers—Thais, rich Khmers, and no foreigners. During the short wait as the plane is prepared for the return flight, I amuse myself examining the five crates of weapons sitting by the landing strip.

Both the flight to, and the landing in Phnom Penh are uneventful. There are not even any policemen to lie to here. I stroll into the domestic arrivals gate and then out to the airport highway without attracting any interest from anyone except the taxi drivers. The ride to Phnom Penh down the familiar 'highway' reveals that most of the battle damage has been repaired, but there is still evidence of the fighting on some walls and fences along the road.

When I reach the Majestic, I am shocked by the emptiness of the place. It had always been busy, with tourists and residents competing for tables. But now, except for a couple of people I vaguely recognize as regulars and two tourists, the place is vacant. I spend the day catching up with acquaintances and absorbing this strange atmosphere of post-coup Phnom Penh.

Rumors
October 15, 1997

Another lackadaisical day at the Majestic. Many of the adventurers have moved on. Some have drifted off to neighboring Thailand or Viet Nam. Others seeking more adventure, drugs, and girls, have headed off to South and Central America. While a new generation of adventurers has arrived, the people I know from my previous trips are almost exclusively lifers—the residue of humanity who have nowhere else to go. The main topic of conversation is how the government—in an effort to bolster its image after the coup—has cracked down on the brothels with some, albeit limited, effect. By now, their conversations about shagging and mind-numbing teaching jobs have lost their shocking impact and become merely tedious.

Moral considerations aside, I found the Phnom Penh I first visited a decadent but vibrant, scintillating, fascinating, and interesting place. The decadent and depressed Phnom Penh I find now is nothing but sad.

Joe is in town on a visit from Kompong Cham, and running into him at the Majestic is a highlight of my visit. He relays some interesting reports about the coup; "There're unproved rumors of Vietnamese soldiers in Phnom Penh during the fighting. One journalist swears he overheard a soldier shouting in Vietnamese into his radio. But some of the CPP guys might've been using Vietnamese as code. I doubt any of the FUNCINPEC troops would've learned any. Another reporter—this guy's considered reliable, claims he'd been taking shots of soldiers with no problems, until he came to this one particular group. They didn't quite look Khmer, and when he went over to get another picture, they turned and went toward another group of soldiers. These guys ran over, took his camera and told him to fuck off. There're some other nasty stories. One guy told me he was looking out his hotel window and saw two truckloads of blue-uniformed bodies being taken in the direction of a wat. Remember blue was the uniform of the KR who defected to Ranaridh. The KR have always been crazy, but nobody fights to the last man. Later we heard there'd been massacres and then quick crema- tions."

I mention the press reports I've seen in Thailand about executions and the discovery of bodies of senior FUNCINPEC officials. *"Yeah, the killing of those senior guys seemed to have stopped pretty soon after the fighting. A lot of friends of mine were terrified after the coup that they'd be next. It seems like the forty or so were the extent of it, at least for now."*

In general, Joe explains, the mood in Cambodia is domi- nated by the economic slump that has hit the country since the coup. Tourism revenue is non-existent, aid money has been halted, and what little foreign investment was planned has largely dried up. There is less money floating around, and a lot of people are losing their jobs. The government is basi- cally broke, and large segments of the army and civil service have not been paid since July. Joe reports positively that the unofficial toll checkpoints on Cambodian highways are no longer tolerated by the central government, and that the prowling pickup trucks of soldiers are not so prevalent on the streets of Phnom Penh.

Joe will be returning to Kompong Cham early tomorrow. He says good-bye, leaving me to a tedious and sad conversa- tion with Dick, who has just arrived at the table. He is telling me about how wonderful it was after the coup but before the brothels closed. In the economic slump after the coup, there were so few foreigners or rich Khmers that he had his pick of prostitutes.

Tee-ya-hee-un K'mow (The Black Soldiers)
October 19, 1997

I am not disappointed to leave Phnom Penh. Boarding the plane to Koh Kong involves even fewer formalities than the trip here and, again, the flight is uneventful. When we land, only a moto driver is interested in my arrival. He tries to charge me a tourist fare, but relents with a smile when I inform him that I will be paying the local price, thank you very much. That settled, we chat amicably during the ride to town. He tells me, smiling, without complaint or self-pity, about his family's experiences under Loon Nol, Pol Pot, and Hun Sen—all the usual tragedies of Cambodia. The episode reminds me yet again of how tolerant the Khmer people are, and how mercilessly their leaders have betrayed them. We arrive in town and, with an unexpected lump in my throat, I hand over twice his original request.

At the waterfront, I notice motorboat drivers clustered around a foreigner. Alex, a young American traveler, has come to Cambodia from Viet Nam. He has no Thai visa, has only a small amount of money to last him until he can change his travelers checks, and is looking for someone to take him to Thailand. He has convinced himself that he can show up in Thailand with no visa and somehow find a way to change his travelers checks in Trat and then make his way to Bangkok "to straighten it all out." The Khmers continually mention the "black soldiers," which I soon learn refers to the Thai border patrol. The Khmers are nervous about getting fined and possibly even imprisoned by the black soldiers as happens (infrequently) on some trips to Thailand.

As the Khmers refuse to take someone without a visa to the Hat Lek pier, Alex asks about getting dropped off on some deserted beach. They are all unenthusiastic, again citing the black soldiers. Finally, one driver who claims to know the coastal area well offers to take Alex and drop him off "in the jungle." We should contact him in the afternoon to see if his wife will let him go.

Presently, John wanders over and the three of us retire to his house. In a remarkably calm posture for someone who is in quite a jam, Alex joins John at the bong. I conclude that my own chances of getting into Thailand will be better if I show up before Alex has a chance to sour everyone's mood at the border. Thanking John for his hospitality, I leave him as I found him, the picture of almost-wholesome contentment.

Back at the waterfront, the motorboat drivers quickly understand that my own request is much simpler than that of the other foreigner this morning. The return trip is identical to the first, except that going in this direction offers a pleasant view of Thailand's coastal islands in the distance. As the casino comes into view, I ready myself for the upcoming engagement with the black soldiers.

The motorboat swings alongside a small rock jetty and I jump off. Where the jetty meets the beachfront is a small shack manned by soldiers. Smiling broadly and waving my passport, I approach the shack. In shockingly bad Thai, I explain that, "I want go Cambodia but go Cambodia cannot. So I come back Thailand." My passport backs up my story that I was unsuccessful in entering Cambodia, and thus never really left Thailand.

After going through my bags in the most thorough check I've ever experienced, the soldiers allow me to (re)enter Thailand. The journalist in me wants to ask them why they believed my story, but a sense of pragmatism wins out and I remain silent. Moving up to the main road, I find a stand for pickup-buses like the one that brought me here from Trat. I recognize one of the Khmers from the motorboat. She tells the rest of the passengers, who all speak Khmer, how the soldiers at the checkpoint laughed uncontrollably at my Thai once I had passed through.

The bus soon has enough passengers, and departs. A couple of minutes out of the bus stand we hit another checkpoint. The officer in charge speaks good English and he wants to know the full details of my visa status. I proudly show him my perfectly valid Thai visa and entry stamp from my arrival in Bangkok two months ago. While he inspects the passport thoroughly, I go through my story of unsuccessfully trying to get to Cambodia, finishing with, "So, I'll just spend my holiday in Trat instead." To my amusement, the inspector is disturbed and confused at the fact that my American passport shows that I was born in Israel. But, since he finds no evidence to the contrary, he accepts my story about Cambodia and allows me through. We are soon speeding up the coastal road to Khlong Yai and then Trat. Once we arrive in Trat, I marvel at how this tiny Thai backwater, with its paved streets, 7–11, department store, and four story buildings is so different from Koh Kong. The bus to Bangkok departs in only twenty minutes. Pulling my recently-purchased copy of Brother Enemy out of my bag, I settle in for the five-hour trip home.

Home

> "Eric was right. I got home and the only difference was that people were older and fatter. The worst thing is that they have no idea how boring their lives are."

The extent to which many residents adapted to Phnom Penh's insanity made it difficult to imagine them living happily anywhere else. The Majestic's emptiness immediately raised the question of where all the former Phnom Penh residents were now, and how they would react when transplanted outside of the singular Phnom Penh greenhouse. While their transient nature and erratic lifestyles made keeping in touch somewhat difficult, I was able to collect a fragmentary picture of where they ended up.

While many residents left Phnom Penh, very few settled at "home", if that word is taken to mean their native countries. In letters and conversations, "home" is generally described as little better than purgatory, but with nice food. Eric, who reluctantly left Phnom Penh to attend postgraduate school in Switzerland, sees being home as a necessary evil. He sent Reiner this e-mail right after the coup erupted;

> . . . You lucky bastards. I've been watching the news reports about Cambodia. I can't believe you guys are actually there while I'm stuck here in Switzerland. I'm homesick for Cambodia. It's stifling here. No 13-year-

old girls, no drugs, no long rides on the motorbike. Anyway, I'll stop writing because I'm tired now. It's disgusting. In Switzerland you actually have to work hard to earn money, and there is not any smack to give you energy when you need it. I just hope that I can survive until December when I come home [Cambodia] for a visit. After that just 18 months and I can leave this hell and begin living again.

See you all soon, Eric.

Other letters from "home" tell similar stories. In June, after Henrik and Nga had fallen in love—but before she left the brothel to live with him—Henrik went home to Denmark for what he expected would be a four month stint. Steve shows me the letter he received from Henrik early in his stay;

Dear Steve,

I'm going crazy here in Denmark. Everything is so dull and I can't get Nga out of my head. I was so extatic when she finally wrote me to say that she was waiting for me. I was suposed to stay in Denmark for four months, but I'm coming back as soon as I sell some stuff for money to return.

I talked with my family about Nga. They know she's a prostatute and has no education. Still, my mother is so exited that I might actually find a wife. She said that if I marry Nga, she will give us $20,000 which would be great to buy a house or somthing.

I'll tell you one strange story. Mostly, my trip was as celibat as I expected. Eric was correct when he said that, "You will get to know your right hand very intimatly." But Julia, this girl I knew from before, started really pressing me at a party. I figured I was completely out of practice in seducing a straigt woman. Besides, after shagging Nga and all the others, I was hardly going to get exited about some large Danish girl with hair under her armspits. Maybe that's

179

what turned her on, me being so indifferent. Anyway, she kept pressing until I gave in. She's a lot older than me, 33 and as soon as we started in bed she was teezing me about the age difference. After we finished, I was just having conversation. I told her about my good-bye party in Svay Pa, when I took those two girls in together. Julia got really upset at me when I told her, "You know Julia, it's funny. The last time I had sex was with two girls. One was 16 and the other 17. So, if you add their ages together, they're also 33, just as you. Isn't that hilarious?" I couldn't believe it, she started sobbing.

Anyway, I am so happy that I will soon be back in Cambodia where things are not so incredably dull like they are here. If you see Nga, please tell her that I am coming back as soon as I can.

Henrik

Even Steve, who has the most ability to be successful in his home country, finds the prospect of settling there intolerable. After being in Cambodia for a year, he has a lot to say about what he finds in the outside world;

Dear Amit,

Being in Bangkok after so long in the boonies was pretty weird. I was almost frightened by how fast the bus was traveling. I didn't travel faster than 35 miles an hour for the entire year I was in Cambodia. Suddenly, I'm in this huge bus speeding down a six lane highway at 60 miles an hour. And the view of Bangkok! The sight of all those Bangkok high-rises with their windows and airplane lights made me feel like I'd entered some terrifying sci-fi megacity like Blade Runner or Brazil.

I got off the bus at Khao San Road. After our tiny community in Phnom Penh and the occasional tourist, I was awed by the sight of so many backpackers. I met up with an Australian who'd just arrived here after living in Japan.

Bangkok was pristine compared to Phnom Penh, but for him the city was an unholy pig sty.

We went to Patpong for the sex shows. I was quite bored. Bangkok's "outrageous" and "notorious" red light district is a Sunday in church compared with Tool Kok or Svay Pa. The flashing lights and the go-go dancing are kind of fun, but really it just made me nostalgic for the simplicity, rawness and, yes I'll use this word, innocence, of Phnom Penh. Plus, the prices. I must have told a hundred touts, "1000 baht [$35 at the time]? Fuck off, it's only 60 in Cambodia." I went to sleep wondering if I'll ever be able to live anywhere else now that I've lived in Phnom Penh.

Eric was right. I got home and the only difference was that people were older and fatter. The worst thing is that they have no idea how boring their lives are. I'm not going to tell them in full. However, they do know that I've visited brothels, and the pictures of Lan raised some eyebrows. But it's nothing they can convict me for.

This guy from my old company became really successful with his own firm. He told me he can't find enough good people and offered to hire me on the spot, and at almost twice the salary of my last job. I was tempted, but I knew it wouldn't be a good idea. After Phnom Penh, could you imagine me at some desk job 10 hours a day, then going home to watch TV because I'm too tired to do anything else? I could last in that for about 3 weeks. And I was thinking, the lifestyle that all that work could buy me—a nice apartment, a maid, drugs, girls, I can get all that in Phnom Penh already. My girlfriend here said I was nuts to turn the job down, but I knew I'd be nuts to accept it.

I noticed something else. It was when people said things like "that party was really outrageous," or "his stag party was pretty wild, huh." These words mean something different for me now: If I use outrageous to describe some beer party, what word can I use to describe an afternoon at Tool Kok? Last week, some friends and I were watching MTV. One particularly 'outrageous' video had the singer in bed with three women. My friends were drooling at the *idea. I didn't tell them that the $15 I had in my wallet will recreate that same scene next time I hit Svay Pa.*

It shouldn't be longer than two or three weeks before I've finally returned to the Promised Land for more fun before joining Lan in Viet Nam.

Cheers, Steve

Australia is not Steve's home, nor was Viet Nam. For his foreseeable future, "home" is to be a series of continuous adventures. At random intervals, he sends me interesting missives from unpredictable parts of the world, such as this wonderful description of Singapore;

What an amazing place, the city where everything works. It's a bit like having dinner at those aristocratic relatives who have you over every once in a while. Everything in their home is perfectly in place, from the manicured lawn to the polished silverware on the table. It is not a house that invites you to play tag or hide and seek. During dinner, the family is well-mannered, friendly, and discusses their investments. It's a pleasant evening, but you look forward to getting home, changing out of your dress clothes, grabbing a beer, and being able to curse when the tab breaks.

I saw a typically Singaporean scene on the spotless and efficient subway. An ad above the well-dressed, serious-looking Singaporeans sitting opposite me read, "Here's what all the fashionable Singaporeans will be wearing this season," followed by face shots of four people of various ages. They are all smiling. That's right, it's part of the government's "Smile Singapore" campaign to encourage its citizens to look friendlier and happier. Looking down and to the left, I saw three signs: No Smoking—Fine $500, No Eating or Drinking—Fine $500, No Littering—Fine $500.

Anyway, I'm definitely impressed with the quality I find in everything Singaporean, but I'm pretty sure I'll never come back.

Other letters have a definite Cambodian flavor. Steve's letter from Romania reads in part;

> *Nothing can beat Phnom Penh, of course, but Bucharest isn't bad. You know I tend to like big girls, and so it was odd for me to be excited about Lan and all those other petite Asians. For size, this is the place to be. The nightclubs are jammed full of these big, blonde, busty Romanian babes. At $25 or $30 for the night, it's not that much more than the girls from the [Street] 154 brothels . . .*

I get similar letters from other adventurers who have left their hearts in Phnom Penh. Letters I receive from South America include these excerpts;

> *You should come out here. Latin women are really hot. Unlike all the lousy shags in Cambodia, these girls samba all over you for an hour and then almost forget to take the money.*

> *What heroin was in Phnom Penh, cocaine is here . . .*

> *You wouldn't believe a place with more guns than Phnom Penh, but I found it . . .*

While some are traveling for the foreseeable future, other Phnom Penh 'emigrés' settle in places more interesting than their countries of origin, but less insane than Phnom Penh. Henrik's depressed letter to Steve from Denmark is in stark contrast to this letter to me from Viet Nam;

> *Dear Amit,*

> *The secret to a happy life is this: When you are single, live in Cambodia. Then get married and live in Viet Nam. I'm off the front lines now. I've axepted my position in the rear eshelons gracefully, but I'm sure I will return for some reserve duty.*

*The really important news is that Nga is pregnant!!!
She'll have the baby in March. You see, it will be a 'coup
baby.' We already have a nice little apartment which we
bought with the money from my mother. After the
crazyness that happened to both of us in Phnom Penh, it's
really nice for the two of us to just relax with each other in
Saigon.*

*Before we moved here, Steve and Lan were living in
the same guesthouse as us. Steve liked Saigon at first, but
soon he started understanding how badly people where
cheeting him. Like the time he and Lan went to Nha Trang
and somone stole their shoes off the beach. All the Vietnamese said they had no idea what happened. They just
gave that Vietnamese smile which means they're lying and
they don't care that you know it. About a week later, the
police showed up and hasled Lan about living with a
foreiner. It was a good thing that I saw and came over,
because Steve would have punched one of the policemen.
The next day he and Lan figured that even though they
loved each other, it was better for Steve to leave. So they
had a tearful goodby and Steve left her with enough money
to last for a long time.*

*So where did Steve go? He's off to Bucharest. He prom-
ised to let me know his address and how he is doing. I
hope that you can come to Saigon when the baby is born.*

All the Best, Henrik.

Running into Gary in Bangkok provides another picture of a
settled happiness, though of a different sort. Gary does not expect to ever return to the US. "I'm teaching in Japan. Working
very hard and sleeping with a lot of girls," he tells me in his
typical matter-of-fact way. The money is great, but the real benefit for Gary is that young Japanese girls seem to have a special fetish for seducing white English teachers. Now he has taken
a holiday and is looking forward to "pink-shopping" (brotheling)
in Phnom Penh for a couple weeks. He expects to continue this
wonderful life cycle for his remaining years. "I make money

working like a dog in Japan, where I can also have sex with cute young Japanese girls, and then just relax, zone out and shag even younger girls for a month in Phnom Penh."

Equally excited about his new adopted home is Reiner. While sitting in a cafe in Bangkok's backpacker ghetto, I hear Reiner's booming voice postulating on Vietnamese perfidy and Khmer insanity from across the street. He tells me he is living in Thailand now. "There's something missing in Cambodia now. There's a sense of hopelessness and defeat in the people. And no tourists or aid money, so everyone's business is down. And that looting really bothered me. I'd been thinking of getting a new computer. Imagine if I'd bought it and then a week later teenagers with guns carry it away. Remember the airport? That really depressed me."

He has few regrets about leaving, though, because the conditions are perfect to make millions exporting gems from Thailand. Having given up on both Viet Nam and Cambodia, I wonder how long it will take Reiner to become disillusioned with Thailand. I take his phone number in Bangkok and we make plans to meet again.

While many expats I got to know left Phnom Penh, there was a sizable contingent who remained even after the coup. A surprise visit from Joe is an opportunity to hear about them. Joe himself had committed to continuing his work in Cambodia despite his dislike of the new government. This was not to be. He has a defeated but determined look on his face as he tells me, "I suppose I was asking for it. I just kept talking to my students about human rights and democracy. One of them reported me to the local CPP officials, and that was it. Hun Neng [the older brother of Hun Sen and the governor of Kompong Cham province] himself called up the NGO director and told her that either I stop working for them, or he shuts the whole operation down. Of course, that means the director and all her officers lose their fat expat salaries. Within the hour, within the goddamn hour, I'm hauled before the director, given a bollocking for breaking the rules by talking about politics, and told that she's called Immigration to revoke my work visa. I guess I should have been more careful since the coup. But they need to learn about human rights now more than ever. If shit like this can happen, we're just headed for another Burma."

Then he hits me with another surprise. "It's actually good that we're leaving. Pholla is pregnant. I can't really imagine raising a child in Cambodia—not before the coup, and especially not now. My child won't be raised by a father whose close friends stop on their way home from work to pay teenagers for sex. My kid won't live next door to neighbors who betray their country and their ideals for a few thousand dollars and have grenade-toting bodyguards."

After discussing the plans he has for living with Pholla in New Zealand, Joe updates me on some of the others who have stayed in Cambodia. Dick lost yet another job, but soon found a new position at one of the dwindling number of Phnom Penh schools he has yet to be fired from. Joe ruefully begins describing his last conversation with Dick. I stop him and pull out my notes for Joe to read. Joe's conversation with Dick, about how Cambodia is now more than ever a buyer's market for paid sex, is identical to the one I had with him during my visit to Phnom Penh.

Joe also tells me about Dirk, who paid $300 to have his girlfriend's abusive husband murdered and then fled the country in fear. "He went to Viet Nam saying he'd never come back to Cambodia. A month later, I saw him at the Majestic. He told me how he couldn't get a job in Viet Nam, how the prostitutes were all overpriced, and how they kept ripping him off, and how 'uptight' all the foreigners there were. 'But I thought you were never coming back to Cambodia,' I said to him. So he says, 'Show me a better place, and I'll go there.'"

Next, Joe shows me a letter and gives me the story behind it. Mike, who simply stopped going to classes shortly before the coup, could not be bothered to find a new job. For a couple of months, he survived by borrowing money from Khmer and foreign friends. But that money dried up as it became clear that Mike was taking no steps to repay his debts. For the third time in the year since he arrived in Cambodia, he was saved from disaster by a wire transfer from his brother who, as opposed to Mike, went to university, has a secure job with an insurance company, and intends to marry his fiancee in the near future.

The letter is a result of his brother's demand for an explanation of what Mike is doing in Cambodia. Mike gave his brother a pretty accurate rundown of the life he and his friends lead in Phnom Penh. He wrote glowingly of the adventures possible in Cambodia and invited his brother to come and experience them for himself. His brother's reaction shows how far from home Mike has strayed.

Dear Michael,

I'm exhausted tonight so I'll be brief. I received your letter and I wish you'd never sent it to me. It makes me regret you ever went there. I find your letter disgusting. Your intentions are evident by your obsession with Champagne and the brothels. Find your soul again, come back to this country and get on with a life an adult should live. Don't imagine that your being "in a different culture" exonerates you in any manner from the acts which you described. I find it a callow posturing. You claim enigmatically that in Cambodia things are acceptable that would never be considered in England and that is no excuse.

I'm sorry for being so harsh, but I look for an attachment for issues surrounding my life besides the fact that I could work 4 hours a day and make enough for a weekend "shagfest."

I'm not in Cambodia. No doubt I would be doing many of the things described. However, if traveling on business without Monica [his fiancee] has taught me anything, it is that just because you can doesn't mean you should. Perhaps it begins with the decision to go to the place. Who knows? Probably you better than me.

Good luck getting out of Cambodia. Hope to see you soon.

Alistair.

Off the Rails in Phnom Penh

I asked about Mike's reaction to the letter. "He was glad his brother had already wired the money. He realized he'd have a hard time getting any more." Mike took the dramatic steps of lowering his rent by moving back to the Majestic and finding a job. Hangovers have resulted in only two missed morning classes so far. One year after I first met Mike, the only discernible difference in him is that his visa is even more out of date and he is deeper in debt to his brother.

Joe concludes giving me the updates and then explains that Pholla is waiting for him. "I don't want her to worry that I'm meeting my Thai girlfriend for a quick shag, which would be quite a feat, because I've never been to Thailand before. But that doesn't prove anything for Pholla." I wish Joe the best and hope that he can continue fighting for what he believes, even if no one in Cambodia seems willing to.

After Joe leaves, I ponder the irony. Joe finds himself unable to survive in Cambodia. But Dick, Dirk, and Mike, are doing well in Cambodia—or at least doing better there than they could anywhere else. Joe, a hardworking, moral, conscientious human being who believes passionately in improving the lot of Cambodians must leave Cambodia. Dick, Dirk, and Mike—who can generously be described as a pathetic loser, a complete flake, and a clueless ne'er-do-well, remain in Cambodia. Given the tragicomic absurdity of Phnom Penh, there is something quite appropriate in that.

Bibliography

Phnom Penh Post. Subscription information for the bi-weekly paper is available at subscription.pppost@worldmail.com.kh.

Bit, Seanglim. *The Warrior Heritage: A Psychological Perspective of Cambodian Trauma*. El Cerrito, CA: Self-Published, 1991.

Carney, Timothy and Tan Lian Choo. *Whither Cambodia?: Beyond the Election*. Singapore: Institute of Southeast Asian Studies, 1993.

Chanda, Nayan. *Brother Enemy*. New York: Macmillan Publishing Co., 1986.

Chandler, David P. *A History of Cambodia*. Boulder: Westview Press, 1996.

Chandler, David P. *Brother Number One: A Political Biography of Pol Pot*. Boulder: Westview Press, 1992.

Chang, Pao-Min. *Kampuchea Between China and Vietnam*. Singapore: Singapore University Press, 1986.

Corfield, Justin J. *Khmers Stand Up!: A History of the Cambodian Government 1970–1975*. Clayton, Australia: Monash University Centre of Southeast Asian Studies, 1994.

Hildebrand, George C. *Cambodia: Starvation and Revolution*. New York: Monthly Review Press, 1990.

Kiernan, Ben. *How Pol Pot Came to Power: A History of Communism in Kampuchea, 1930–1975*. London: Verso, 1985.

Shawcross, William. *Sideshow: Kissinger, Nixon and the Destruction of Cambodia*. New York: Chatto and Windus, 1979.

Szymusiak, Molyda. *The Stones Cry Out: A Cambodian Childhood, 1975–1980*. New York: Hill and Wang, 1986.

Vickery, Michael. *Cambodia 1975–1982*. Boston: South End Press, 1984.